Europe
Teacher/Parent Notes

The purpose of this book is to help young people become more familiar with Europe through reading, writing, researching, and illustrating. They can then share the information they discover with classmates, friends, and family.

Present as much information as possible about a specific region or country before having students complete the related activity sheets. Have available encyclopedias and other reference books so that the students can accomplish the research necessary to complete the activity sheets. They may find the *World Book Encyclopedia* to be most helpful. Teachers/Parents are encouraged to add information on other locations, points of interest, rivers, and so on, when working on the mapping activities.

The following methods may be used to integrate this book into your curriculum:

Independent Activities

Each student may work on the activity sheets of his/her choice. The activity sheets can be stored in a folder. After all of the materials for a specific country have been completed, the teacher/parent should have a conference with the student to go over the materials together. If any information is incorrect, help the student locate the correct answers. The materials may then be stapled into a booklet.

Small Group Activities

The students may be divided into small groups to work on the specific countries of Europe. After a group has completed the work, they may share their information with the other groups. Creative presentations should be encouraged. For example, one group may decide to present their findings through a simple play, while another group may share what they have learned through an imaginary travelogue.

Large Group Activities

You may wish to have the entire class or a large group work on certain pages, displaying the chosen pages on an overhead projector and working through the pages together.

Special Note

Advise students to remain alert to current events taking place in Europe. You might maintain an ongoing bulletin board to display newspaper and magazine articles which relate to European countries.

Name ____________________

Physical Features

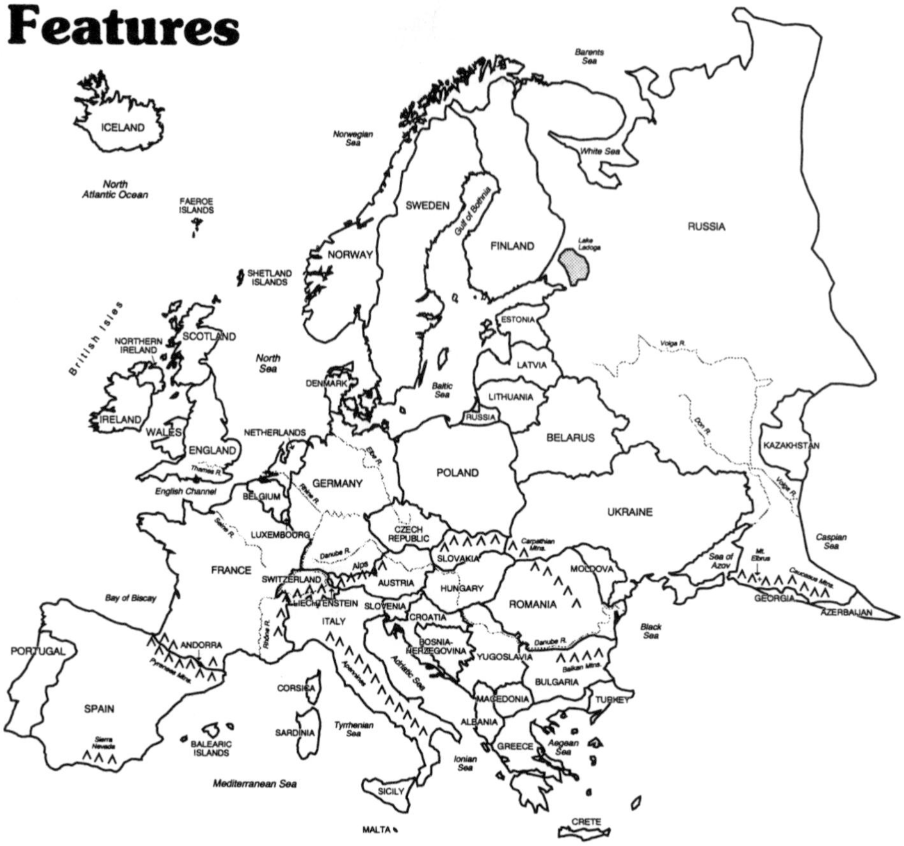

1. What is Europe's longest river? ____________________
2. What are the four major land regions of Europe?

   ____________________ ____________________

   ____________________ ____________________

3. What is a peninsula? ____________________

   ____

4. List the five major European peninsulas.

   ____________________ ____________________

   ____________________ ____________________

   ____

5. What is Europe's largest lake? ____________________

   Describe its water. Why is it considered a lake? ____________________

   ____

Extension: Choose a topic such as Europe's climate, landforms, or plant and animal life to research and study. Share your information through a story, report, travel guide, or art activity.

Name ______________________________

History and Culture

1. Scientists have found fossils indicating that humans lived in Europe how many years ago?

   ____

2. Where did the first civilizations develop? ______________________________

   ____

3. What is another name for the Black Death? ______________________________

   When did it first break out in Europe and how many people did it kill?______________________________

   ____

4. When did the period known as the Renaissance begin? ______________________________
5. When did the great age of European discovery begin? ______________________________
6. What is the Helsinki agreement? ______________________________

   ____

7. How many languages are spoken in Europe? ______________________________
8. How many countries are in Europe? ______________________________
9. Use a current atlas or encyclopedia to find recent population figures of Europe. What country has the largest population? How many people live there?

   ____

   What country has the smallest population? How many people live there? ______________________________

   ____

10. What are autobahns? ______________________________

    ____

11. What is Europe's oldest airline? ______________________________
12. What is Telstar I? ______________________________

    ____

Extension: Make a time line of events from the European Renaissance.

Name ______________________

Physical Features

1. On the map, draw a star to mark the location of the capital of Albania. Write the city's name next to the star.
2. Label the sea and three countries that border Albania.
3. List the country's major rivers that empty into the sea. Draw a star by the only one used for shipping.

   ____

   ____

   ____

   ____

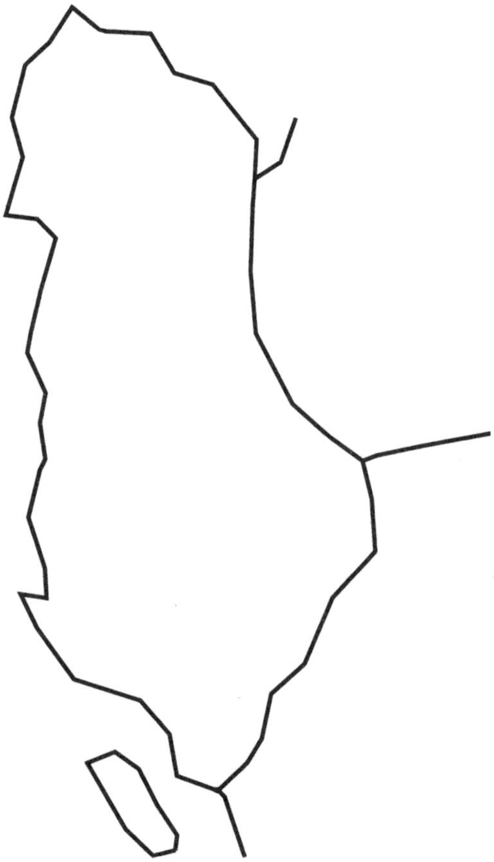

4. Draw in the North Albanian Alps on the map using ^^^.
5. Draw a triangle to show where the highest elevation is located. What is the name of

   this mountain? ______________

   What is its elevation in feet? __________

   in meters? __________
6. List four minerals that are mined in Albania.

   ______________________ ______________________

   ______________________ ______________________
7. For many years Albania's borders were closed. People were allowed neither in nor out of the country. How do you think this policy was enforced?

   ____

   ____

   ____

   When was this policy changed? ______________________

Extension: Research the climate of Albania. Explain in a short report how the mountains affect its weather.

Name ____________________

History and Culture

1. In the box, draw and correctly color the flag of Albania.
2. What is the name of the ancient tribe that ruled Albania in 300 B.C.?

   ____

3. List six of the major civilizations that influenced Albania during the years from 300 B.C. to A.D. 1300.

   ____

   ____

   ____

   ____

   ____

   ____

4. Who is Albania's national hero? ____________________
5. In recent times, Albania has been occupied by many countries. What country invaded Albania in 1939? ____________________
6. Who is Enver Hoxha? ____________________

   ____

   ____

7. Why do you think so many Albanians disliked Communist rule?

   ____

   ____

   ____

   ____

   ____

   ____

Extension: Albania has many different cultural influences. List three of the ways this could benefit a country. Share with your classmates.

Name ______________________

Physical Features

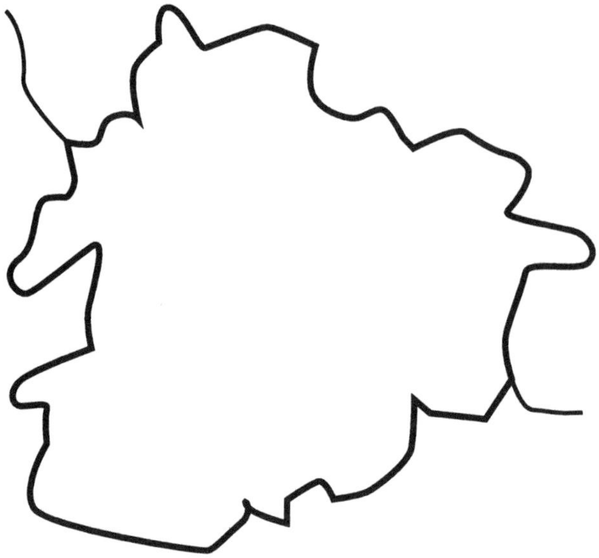

1. Mark the location of the capital of Andorra on the map with a star. Write the city's name next to the star.
2. Label the countries that border Andorra.
3. What is the area of Andorra in square miles? ______________________
4. Name a European country that is smaller in area than Andorra.

   ____

   How many square miles smaller is it than Andorra?______________________
5. Why have Andorra's boundaries changed little?

   ____

   ____

   ____

   ____

   ____
6. Label the Pyrenees Mountains using ^^^ on the map. Draw a triangle at the location of Andorra's highest peak. Write the name of the peak near the triangle.
7. Andorra's climate is ______________________. The average winter temperatures range from ____________ to ____________. The summer temperatures range from ____________ to ____________.
8. What is Andorra's leading agricultural product? ______________________

Extension: Tobacco threatens the health of those who use it. What could a person do to discourage farmers from growing tobacco? Make a list of at least three ways to do this, and share your ideas with your classmates.

Name ____________________

History and Culture

1. Andorra has a national and a state flag. In the boxes provided on this page, draw and correctly color each flag.
2. What is the official language of Andorra?

   ____

3. Until 1993, Andorra was ruled by which two heads of state? What country did each represent?

   ____

   ____

   What was the name given these rulers?

   ____

   When did the two countries begin jointly ruling Andorra? ____________________
4. Under Andorra's new constitution, who now heads Andorra's government?

   ____

5. When did women win the right to vote in Andorra? ____________________

   How many years is this after women in the United States gained the right to vote?

   ____

6. Name Andorra's chief means of income.

   ____

national flag

state flag

Extension: What problems do you think might occur when two countries jointly rule another country? Incorporate your ideas into a short story or skit. Or design a poster that details the differences between the two ruling countries.

Name ______________________

Physical Features

1. On the map, draw a star to indicate the location of Austria's capital. Write the city's name next to the star.
2. Draw and label Austria's longest river.
3. Austria is a landlocked country. What is the definition of landlocked?____________

    ____

    ____

    How many countries border Austria? _____ Label them on the map.
4. List and briefly describe Austria's six main land regions.

    ____
    ____
    ____
    ____
    ____
    ____
    ____
    ____
5. Despite Austria's mountainous terrain, it manages to grow enough crops to supply three-quarters of the food needed by its people. Which of Austria's regions is most used for farming?

    ____
6. What are the major influences on Austria's climate? ______________________________

    ____
    ____
    ____

Extension: Research and then write a report on a well-known river, mountain range, or other physical feature in Austria.

Name ______________________

General Information

1. What is Austria's official language? ______________________

   List three other countries that share this language.

   ____

2. Austria is a neutral country. Define the word *neutral* and tell how Austria's neutrality is shown.

   ____

   ____

   ____

3. What is the English meaning of the following words?

   chalet: ______________________________________

   dirndl: ______________________________________

   Wiener schnitzel: ______________________________

4. Austrians enjoy many sports. List at least four. ______________________

   ____

5. Explain the three options available to students who want to complete their education at a university. ______________________________

   ____

   ____

6. Describe Austrian work conditions. Include information on vacations and the length of the workday and workweek.

   ____

   ____

   ____

Extension: Choose an Austrian sport to research and study. Then share your knowledge through a short story or report.

Name ____________________

History and Culture

1. In the box, draw and correctly color Austria's flag.
2. What is the title of Austria's national anthem?

   ____

   ____

3. When did the Thirty Years' War begin?

   ____

   Briefly tell what the war was about.

   ____

   ____

4. What was the Salic law?

   ____

   ____

5. Who was Austria's first woman ruler? ______________________________
6. What did Austria do in 1955 to obtain independence? ______________________

   ____

7. Who was Mozart? ____

   List some of his works. ______________________________________

   ____

   ____

8. What Austrian was famous for his waltzes? ____________________________
9. What is the meaning of the word *baroque*? ____________________________

   ____

10. Who is one of Austria's best-known baroque architects?

    ____

Extension: Choose an Austrian artist or musician to research. Find a recording or picture of their work and share it with your class.

Name ____________________

Physical Features and General Information

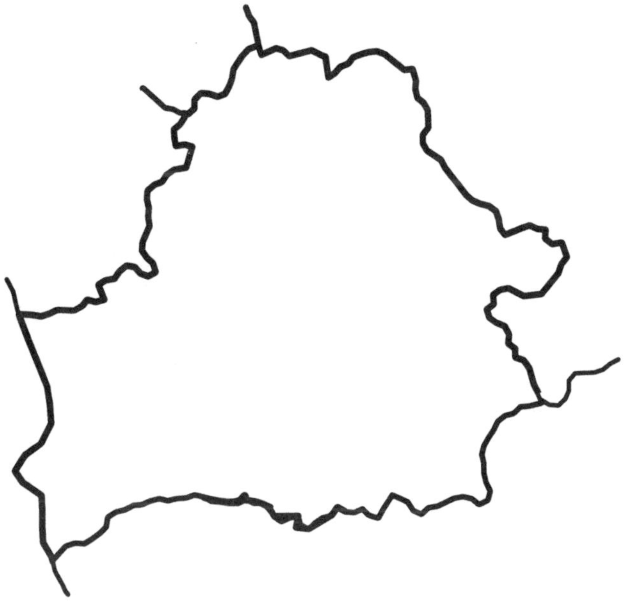

1. On the map, draw a star to show the location of the capital. Write the city's name by the star.
2. Label the countries that border Belarus.
3. Most of the land in Belarus is ______________________________.
4. Belarus has over ________________ small lakes.
5. List the country's four major rivers.

    ____

    ____

    ____

    ____
6. Belarus declared its independence from Soviet rule in ________________.
7. What is the country's official language? ______________________________
8. What happened in Ukraine in 1986? How did this event affect Belarus? ______________

    ____

    ____

    ____
9. What is the education level of most Belarusians? ______________________________

    ____
10. List the crafts for which Belarus is known. ______________________________

    ____
11. Briefly describe the lifestyle of the Belarus people.

    ____

    ____

    ____

    ____

Name ____________________

Physical Features

1. On the map, draw a star to indicate the location of the capital of Belgium. Write the city's name next to the star.
2. Label the four countries and the body of water that border Belgium.
3. Using the population guide in an encyclopedia, find Belgium's three largest cities other than the capital. Show their locations on the map using dots. Write each city's name by its dot.
4. Draw and label the four main land regions. Write a brief description of each.

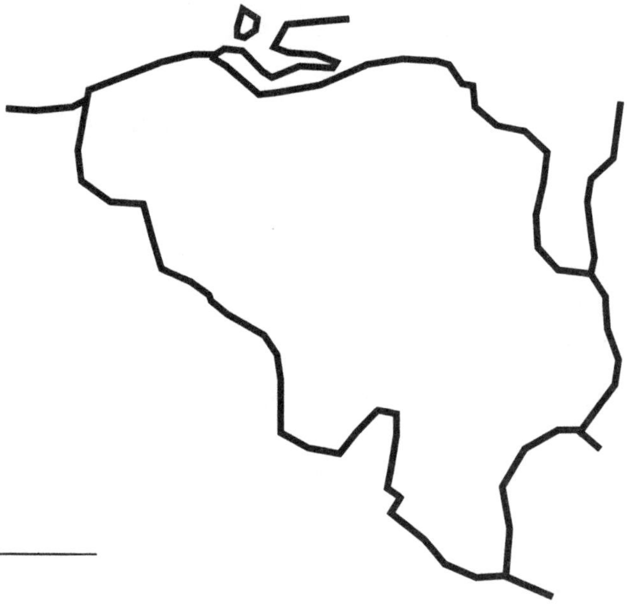

5. What is a *polder*? ____________________

Where are polders found in Europe besides Belgium?

6. Describe Belgium's climate and tell how it benefits the country.

Name ______________________

History and Culture

1. In the box, draw and correctly color Belgium's flag.
2. What is Belgium's national anthem?

 ____

 ____

3. Who gave Belgium its name?

 ____

 ____

4. Where did Napoleon's final defeat occur?

 ____

5. In 1865, Belgium established the Congo Free State in central Africa. By what name was it known in 1908? ______________________

 What is it known as today? ______________________

6. What are the two major groups of people in Belgium?

 ______________________ ______________________

 List three ways in which these two groups differ from one another.

 Group 1: ______________________ *Group 2:* ______________________

 ______________________ ______________________

 ______________________ ______________________

 ______________________ ______________________

7. Briefly describe the Belgians' diet.

 ____

 ____

8. Belgium has two school systems. What are they called?

 ______________________ ______________________

9. Name the two famous Belgium surrealist painters from the early 20th century.

 ______________________ ______________________

Extension: Belgium has many famous artists. Choose one on which to do additional research. Share what you learned through a story, report, play, poster, or other project.

Name ______________________

Physical Features and General Information

1. On the map, draw a star to show the location of Bosnia's capital. Write the city's name by the star.
2. Describe the country's two land regions.

   ____

   ____

   ____

   How do the two differ?

   ____

   ____

   ____

3. Draw and label the country's four major rivers. Label the countries that border Bosnia-Herzegovina.
4. Draw a ∧ to show the country's highest point. Print its name next to the symbol. What is its elevation?____________ feet ____________ meters
5. Bosnia's mountainous land and cold, snowy winters make it a perfect place for ____________ . Sarajevo hosted the Winter Olympics of what year? ____________
6. From 1918 to 1992, Bosnia was part of a kingdom of Serbs, Croats, and Slovenes who formed what came to be called ______________________ through most of the century. Bosnia declared its independence from this nation in 1992 against the wishes of the ______________ who declared war on all non-Serbs.
7. Define *ethnic cleansing* as it refers to the struggle in Bosnia. ______________________

   ____

   ____

8. Most people in Bosnia speak ______________________ . However, Serbs use the ______________ alphabet while Muslims, Croats, and others use the ______________ alphabet.

Extension: Research the conflict in Bosnia-Herzegovina by paging through recent news magazines. Make a list of seven things those involved in the conflict could do to prevent such a bloody struggle from ever occurring again.

Name ______________________

Physical Features

1. On the map, draw a star to show the location of Bulgaria's capital. Write the city's name next to the star.
2. Label the countries that border Bulgaria.
3. What sea borders Bulgaria to the east?

   ____

   Label it on the map.
4. What is the largest mountain range that covers Bulgaria?

   ____
5. Mark the highest peak with the symbol ^ and write its name beside the symbol.
6. What are Bulgaria's two leading grain crops? ______________________
7. Name and briefly describe Bulgaria's four land regions.

   ____

   ____

   ____

   ____
8. Why does Bulgaria's climate vary so much from region to region?

   ____

   ____
9. Where is Bulgaria's most popular vacation area? Why?

   ____

   ____

   ____

Extension: Pretend you are climbing Bulgaria's highest peak. Write a story about your climb. Include such details as what you will bring and how long your climb will take.

Name ______________________

History and Culture

1. In the box, draw and color the flag. How has it changed in the last few years?

____
____
____

2. Why were the Thracians important to Bulgaria's history?

____
____
____
____

3. How long did Turkish rule last in Bulgaria? ______________________
4. Why did Bulgaria enter World War I and World War II?

____
____
____

5. By what year was Bulgaria totally controlled by the Communists? ____________
6. List some of the minority groups that make up Bulgaria.

______________________ ______________________
______________________ ______________________

7. What is Bulgaria's official language? ______________________

   To what other language is it similar? ______________________
8. Bulgaria has a literacy rate of 98 percent. Define *literacy*.

____
____

Extension: Read about the Bulgaria of today in newspapers and current news magazines. Incorporate this information into a poster that compares the old Bulgaria with the new.

Name ____________________

Physical Features and General Information

1. On the map, draw a star to show the location of Croatia's capital. Write the city's name by the star.
2. List and describe Croatia's two land regions.

   ____

   ____

   ____

   ____

   ____

   ____
3. The ______________ Alps run through the country's center. Mark them on the map using the symbol ^^^.
4. What is a *bora*? ______________________________

   ____
5. Why did war break out in 1991? ______________________________

   ____

   ____
6. What are the two major ethnic groups in Croatia? ______________________________
7. ______________ is the official language and is actually so much like ______________ that some linguists consider them dialects of a single language called ______________ .

   How do these two language forms differ and why do you think Croats wish to distinguish them further? ______________________________

   ____

   ____
8. How did the recent war affect where Croats live? ______________________________

   ____
9. How has rock music played a role in recent Croatian history? ______________________________

   ____

Name ____________________

Physical Features

1. On the map, draw a star to show the location of the capital of the Czech Republic. Write the city's name by the star.
2. Label the four countries that border the Czech Republic.
3. Name the country's five land regions.

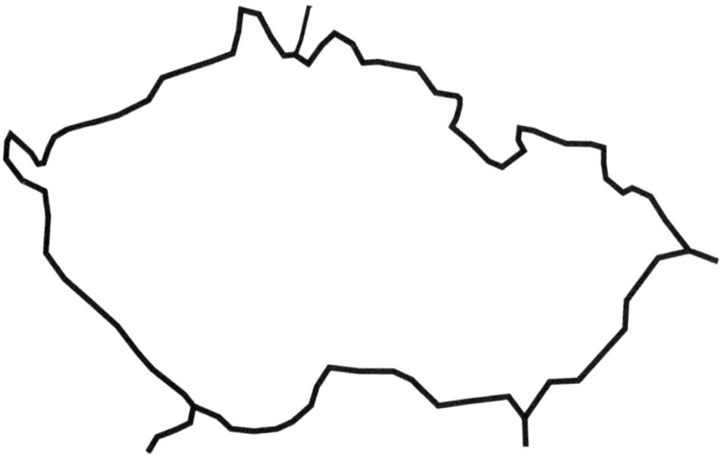

____

____

____

____

____

Choose one of the regions and write a short description.

____

____

____

4. Name two leading manufacturing cities in the Czech Republic.

______________________________ ______________________________

5. What are some of the major crops grown in this country? List at least four.

____

6. What plagues one of the country's largest nature preserves in the Krkonose Mountains? Where do you think this problem most likely originated?

____

____

____

Extension: Research the Czech Republic's land regions. Then write a travelogue about your trip to one or more of these land regions. Incorporate facts into your travelogue.

Name ______________________

History

1. In the box, draw and correctly color the Czech Republic's flag.
2. When was this area first settled?

   ____

   Who were the first settlers?

   ____
3. What is the Czech Republic's national anthem? ______________________

   ____
4. Who was Alexander Dubcek? ______________________

   ____

   ____
5. The Czech Republic was once part of what country? ______________________

   When did it become independent? ______________________
6. Václav Havel was a non-communist ______________________ who served as ______________________ of the former Czechoslovakia in the early 1990s. Would such a person ever hold this position in your country? Explain. ______________________

   ____

   ____
7. What was the Velvet Revolution and how did it get its name?

   ____

   ____
8. What is the traditional Czech meal at Christmas? ______________________
9. *New Wave* refers to which Czech art of the 1960s? ______________________

   Describe the goal of this art form. ______________________

   ____

Extension: A modern renaissance is occurring in the city of Prague. Research this renaissance in news magazines or other sources and write a skit illustrating it.

Name ____________________

Physical Features

1. On the map, draw a star to show the location of the capital of Denmark. Write the city's name next to the star.
2. Mark the location of Denmark's three largest cities, other than the capital, by drawing a dot with the city's name written next to each.
3. Label the country that borders Denmark.
4. Denmark consists of a large peninsula and many islands. Name the peninsula.

   ____

   Approximatedly how many islands make up Denmark? ____________________
5. Denmark's land is covered by a material called *moraine*. Define moraine.

   ____

   ____
6. Name Denmark's land regions. ____________________

   ____

   ____

   Describe one of these regions. ____________________

   ____

   ____

   ____
7. What is the chief cause of Denmark's mild, damp climate? ____________________

   ____

Extension: Research transportation in Denmark. Then pretend that you are leading a group of bicyclists from Copenhagen to Alborg with a stop in Odense. Trace your route in pencil on the map above. On a separate sheet, tell about your tour. Include answers to the following questions. How many kilometers will you travel? How will you get your bicycles across the Great Belt (channel)?

Name ____________________

History and Culture

1. In the box, draw and correctly color the flag of Denmark.
2. Who was King Harald Bluetooth?

____

____

____

3. What was the Union of Kalmar?

____

____

____

4. Describe Denmark's role in World War II. ____________________

____

____

____

5. What famous person from Denmark wrote fairy tales? ____________________

   List four stories written by this author.

____

____

6. What kind of food is *smørrebrød*? ____________________

____

7. After reading about Denmark, explain why each of the following items could be included in a poster on Denmark.

   a. stork ____________________

   b. Viking ____________________

   c. soccer ball ____________________

   d. Tivoli Gardens ____________________

   e. Storstrøm Bridge ____________________

   f. barley ____________________

   Design a travel poster and include information on at least three of the items.

Name ______________________

Physical Features and General Information

1. On the map, draw a star to indicate the location of the capital of Estonia. Write the city's name next to the star.
2. Label the countries that border Estonia.
3. Label the Baltic Sea, the Gulf of Finland, and the Gulf of Riga.
4. Estonia's land is chiefly a ______________ .
5. Read about the climate of Estonia and explain it in your own words.

   ____

   ____

   ____

   ____

   ____

   ____

   Why is this climate unusual for its location? ______________________________

   ____

   ____

6. Do most Estonians live in urban or rural areas? ______________________________
7. Most Estonians work in ______________________ or ______________________ .
8. In the box, draw and color Estonia's flag. Explain the meaning of each of the colors.

   ____

   ____

   ____

   ____

   ____

   ____

Name ______________________

Physical Features

1. On the map, draw a star to indicate the location of Finland's capital. Write the city's name next to the star.
2. Label the Gulf of Bothnia and the Gulf of Finland.
3. Label the countries that border Finland.
4. Using a dashed line (--------), show where the Arctic Circle crosses Finland. Why is the area inside the Arctic Circle known as the "Land of the Midnight Sun"?

   ____

   ____

   ____

   ____

5. What is the *aurora borealis*?

   ____

   ____

   ____

   ____

   What is another name for the aurora borealis? ______________________________
6. What covers more than two-thirds of the land in Finland? ______________________________
7. What type of power provides half of Finland's electricity? ______________________________
8. List at least two Finnish industries and tell how they relate to Finland's natural resources.

   ____

   ____

   ____

Extension: Choose a specific physical feature of Finland to research. Share your information through an illustrated poster.

Name ________________

History and Culture

1. In the box, draw and correctly color Finland's flag.
2. Who were the first people known to have lived in Finland?

   ____

   When did the ancestors of present-day Finns begin to arrive?

   ____
3. What countries once fought over possession of Finland?

   ____
4. What are the two official languages of Finland? Write the percentage of people who speak each one.

   a. ________________ ______%

   b. ________________ ______%
5. What is Finland's name in Finnish? ________________
6. What is a *sauna*? What has it to do with Finland? ________________

   ____
7. Who was Elias Lönnrot? Why is he important to Finnish culture? ________________

   ____

   ____

   ____
8. List three of the social welfare programs of Finland.

   ____

   ____

   ____
9. Finland is the world's leading producer of what building material? ________________
10. Who is Finland's present head of state? ________________

Name ______________________

Finnish Foods

1. In Finland, kropsu is served at morning and afternoon work breaks, especially to those people working in the fields. Try the recipe below.

Finnish Kropsu

3 large eggs
½ cup sugar
¾ cup flour
¼ teaspoon salt
¼ pound butter or margarine (one stick)
2 cups milk

Beat eggs and sugar until well-blended. Add flour and salt and mix well. Melt the butter in a small sauce pan. Add the melted butter to the batter and beat well. Blend in the milk. Pour the batter into a 9- x 13-inch pan and bake in a 400° oven until browned and set, about 30-40 minutes.

The dough will puff up while cooking but fall when cooling. Cut in squares and eat by hand or serve on a plate. If desired, top with whipped cream and sliced fruit.

2. What are some other Finnish foods? ______________________

____

3. What meat is considered a special treat in Finland? ______________________

Extension: Make up your own Finnish trivia game. Play the game at a Finnish theme party at which Kropsu is served.

Name ________________

Physical Features

1. On the map, draw a star to indicate the location of the capital of France. Write the city's name by the star.
2. Label the countries that border France.
3. Draw and label the three main rivers that run through France.
4. On the map, draw and label the highest mountains in France.
5. How many main land regions are there in France? ________________

   Name and then describe the region in which you would most enjoy living if you were to move to France. Explain why.

   ____

   ____

   ____

   ____

6. What is the Riviera? What affects its climate?

   ____

   ____

   ____

7. Name France's most important natural resource. What is its primary use?

   ____

8. Write the name and give a brief description of one of France's famous caves.

   ____

   ____

   ____

Extension: Pretend that you and a friend have just discovered a new cave. Write a short story about your adventure.

Name ______________________

History and Culture

1. What is the name of France's flag?

   ____

   Draw and correctly color the flag in the box.
2. What is the national anthem?

   ____
3. In ancient times, tribes of Celts and other peoples lived in the region now called France. What did the Romans call this region? ______________________
4. Napoleon Bonaparte was considered an excellent administrator. List at least two reasons why.

   ____

   ____
5. What is the Tour de France? ______________________

   ____
6. Explain how the United States became the home of the French-produced Statue of Liberty.

   ____

   ____
7. Name at least one French painter known for each of the following art styles.

   Impressionism ______________________

   Neoclassicism ______________________

   Romanticism ______________________

   Postimpressionism ______________________

   Surrealism ______________________

   Cubism ______________________

Extension: Draw a picture on another sheet of paper that relates to the culture of France. Use the style of a famous French artist. Name the artist and the style you chose.

Name ______________________

Language

Use a French dictionary, an encyclopedia, or other source to complete the activities below.

1. Write the correct numeral above each French number word. Identify your source.

________ dix	________ un	________ neuf
________ deux	________ huit	________ cinq
________ quatre	________ six	________ trois
________ sept	Source: ________	

2. Write the French number words in the correct order. Add a comma between each number.

____

____

3. Draw at least three objects in the box below and label them in English and in French. You may use the back of this paper if you want to draw and label more objects. Make sure the words are spelled correctly. Learn the correct pronunciations.

Source: ________________________ Page(s): ____________

Name ______________________

Eiffel Tower

1. In which city is the Eiffel Tower located?

   ____

   When was it built? ______________________

   What is its height? ______________________

2. List the Eiffel Tower's features and tell why it was built.

   ____

3. Why do you think the Eiffel Tower is so famous? ______________________

4. Imagine that you are standing by the Eiffel Tower. Describe what you might see and do there.

   ____

Name ____________________

Physical Features

1. On the map, draw a star to show the location of Germany's capital. Write the city's name next to the star. Use dots to show the location of four other German cities. Label each.
2. Label the countries and seas that border Germany.
3. How long is the Rhine River in standard and in metric measurements?

   ____

   Draw and label this river.
4. Briefly describe the Bavarian Alps.

   ____

   ____

   ____

   ____
5. Name Germany's highest peak and give its height.

   ____
6. Name and describe Germany's largest land region.

   ____

   ____
7. Read about the trees in the Black Forest. List two kinds of trees that grow there.

   ____

Extension: Draw and color a leaf and/or branch from each Black Forest tree you listed above. Label each.

Name ____________________

History

1. In the box, draw and correctly color the German flag.

2. What was the Reformation?

3. Briefly describe Germany's role in World War I.

4. When Adolf Hitler came into power, he pursued two goals. What were they? List two or three ways in which he set out to accomplish these goals.

5. Briefly explain when and why the wall was built between East and West Berlin.

Extension: Research the Holocaust and write an essay answering the following: What was the Holocaust? How do you think such a thing could have occurred in this century in a country of well-educated people? Could it happen in your country? Explain.

Name ______________________

Culture

1. Germany's most popular organized sport is ______________________.
2. List at least six other sports or activities Germans enjoy doing during their leisure time.

____

____

3. Write three facts on one of the following German composers: Bach, Beethoven, Brahms, or Wagner. ______________________

____

____

____

Source: ______________________ Page(s): ____________

4. Read about a German artist. Then list the title of one of his art pieces and the name of the museum where it is located.

____

____

5. What was the *Bauhaus*? ______________________

____

____

6. Germany is known for introducing several well-known foods. Name four.

____

7. If you were to visit Germany, what would you like to see or do?

____

____

____

____

____

Extension: Research Neuschwanstein Castle. Find out what is unique about it and design a modern version that also has unusual features. Show a cut-away view of the interior with labels for each room and feature.

Name ______________________

Language

Refer to a German dictionary, an encyclopedia, or other source to complete the activities below.

1. Write the correct numeral above each German number word. List your source.

________ fünf	________ acht	________ ein
________ zehn	________ drei	________ neun
________ zwei	________ sechs	________ vier
________ sieben	Source: ________________	

2. Write the German number words in the correct order. Add a comma between each number.

____

____

3. Draw at least three objects in the box below and label them in English and in German. You may use the back of this page if you want to draw and label more objects. Make sure the words are spelled correctly. Learn the correct pronunciations.

Source: ______________________ Page(s): __________

Name ____________________

Physical Features

1. On the map, draw a star to show the location of Great Britain's capital. Write the city's name by the star.
2. Draw and label the two longest rivers in Great Britain.
3. The official name of this nation is "The United Kingdom of Great Britain and Northern Ireland," but most people call this country one of these three names:

   ____

   ____

   ____

4. What body of water separates Great Britain from France?

   ____

   How has this body of water helped Great Britain?

   ____

   ____

5. Name Great Britain's land regions.

   ____

   ____

   ____

   Pick two of the regions that most interest you and explain why.

   ____

   ____

   ____

   ____

Extension: Research both Great Britain's climate and that of Labrador, Canada. Compare the latitudes of these two places. Why do these two locations have such vastly different climates?

Name ______________________

History

1. In the box, draw and color Great Britain's flag. In what year was it officially adopted?

   ____

2. The national anthem of Great Britain is

   ____

   ________________________________.

3. What is the basic unit of money in Great Britain? ____________________

4. How is the "throne" passed from one person to another in Great Britain?

   ____

   ____

5. How did the Victorian Age get its name?

   ____

   ____

   During the Victorian Age, the British Empire included what fraction of the world's land and people? ____________________

6. List the six large countries that were British colonies up until 1931 when they gained independence. ________________________________

   ____

   These six countries became the first members of the ____________________.

7. Describe Great Britain's role in World War II. ________________________________

   ____

   ____

   ____

8. Which British leader inspired and unified both his people and other allies in the effort to win World War II? ____________________

Name ____________________

Culture

1. The most popular sport in Great Britain is

   ____________________.

   What are some other favorite sports and pastimes of the British?

   ____

   ____

   ____

2. The British Museum in London has many wonderful treasures such as the Rosetta Stone from Egypt and the Elgin Marbles from the Parthenon in Athens. Write a brief description of these two items.

   ____

   ____

   ____

3. What is the largest library in Great Britain? ____________________

4. Identify Great Britain's grammar schools, independent schools, and public schools.

   ____

   ____

   ____

5. Who was William Shakespeare? List two of his works.

   ____

   ____

   ____

6. For what goods are each of the following countries known?

   Wales: ____________________

   England: ____________________

   Scotland: ____________________

   Northern Ireland: ____________________

Extension: The British have made major contributions to rock music. Research a British band and write a magazine article outlining the group's history.

Name ____________________

Big Ben

1. Some tourists who go to Europe want to see Big Ben. What is it?

____

____

2. Big Ben is located in what city? ____________________

3. How did Big Ben get its name?

____

____

____

____

____

4. How much does Big Ben weigh? ____________________

5. Draw the clock face of Big Ben on the tower in the illustration.

6. If you were to travel to Europe, would you like to see Big Ben?

   Why, or why not?____________________

____

____

7. Pretend that you have been given the job of cleaning Big Ben. How would you go about this interesting but challenging task?

____

____

____

____

____

____

Extension: On another sheet, draw a picture of the place that you would most like to visit in Great Britain.

Name ____________________

Physical Features

1. On the map, draw a star to mark the location of the capital of Greece. Write the city's name by the star.
2. Write the names of the following seas on the map where they are located: Aegean, Ionian, Mediterranean, Sea of Crete.
3. What is the Peloponnesus?

   ____

   ____

   ____

   ____

   Label it on the map.
4. Label the countries that border Greece.
5. Of what stone is much of Greece's land composed?____________________
6. What is *maquis*? ____________________

   ____
7. What is Greece's tallest mountain? Write its height in standard and metric measurements.

   ____

   Why is this mountain so famous? ____________________

   ____
8. What makes the island of Ithaca a tourist attraction? ____________________

   ____
9. Write an interesting fact about the Greek islands.

   ____

   Source: ____________________ Page(s): ____________________
10. Choose a specific island, set of islands, river, mountain, coastline, or other physical feature to study and report on to others.

Name ______________________

History and Culture

1. In the box, draw and correctly color the flag. What do the stripes represent?

____

____

____

____

2. Who was the great leader who conquered the Greeks and became their first king in 338 B.C.?

____

3. Who was the son of the above ruler? What was his major accomplishment?

____

____

____

4. List at least two reasons why the Parthenon is highly regarded.

____

____

5. What contributions have the ancient Greek civilization given to our civilization?

____

____

6. What are the *Iliad* and the *Odyssey*? ______________________

____

____

7. Many modern Greeks dance to folk music featuring what two instruments?

____

8. What is the Greek's favorite meat?______________________ List the ingredients found in *dolmathes* and *moussaka*. ______________________

____

Name ____________________

Art

After studying Ancient and Modern Greece, draw pictures representing each period.

Ancient Greece

Modern Greece

Name ______________________

Olympic Games

1. The Olympic Games originated in ancient Greece. What Greek god was honored at the ceremonies?______________________
2. What did a winning participant of the ancient Olympics receive?______________________
3. Why did the ancient Olympics end? When did the modern Olympics begin?

____

____

____

4. Under what name did the athletes from the group of former Soviet states compete under in 1992? ______________________
5. Imagine you have just won a gold medal. What sport did you win it in? Write a short story or report about your Olympic experience.

Extension: Pick a European country that has competed in the Olympics. Research the events, athletes, or special occurrences of a specific year. Present your findings by reenacting a portion of that year's Olympic Games.

Name ______________________

Physical Features

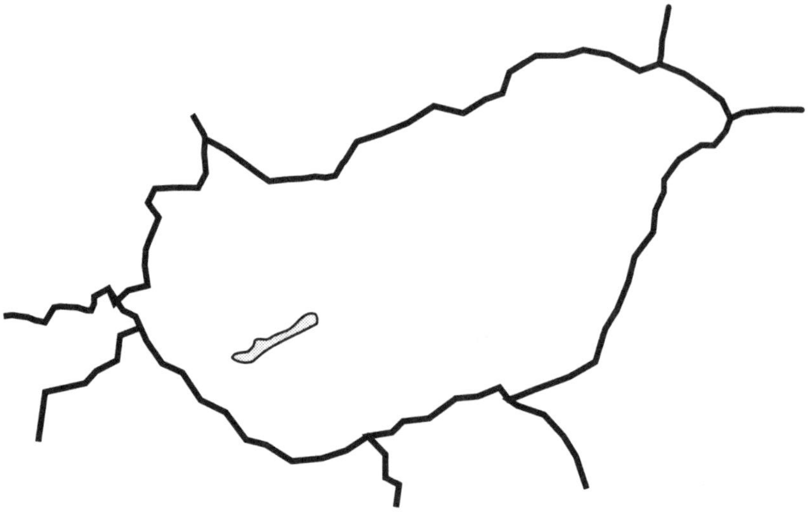

1. On the map, draw a star to mark the location of the capital of Hungary. Write the city's name by the star.
2. Label the countries that border Hungary.
3. On the map, draw and label the Danube River. Write three facts about this river.

____

____

____

____

____

____

4. Name and describe the largest lake in Hungary. Label it on the map.

____

____

5. List the names of the four main land regions of Hungary:

__________________________ __________________________

__________________________ __________________________

Choose one of these regions and write a brief description.

____

____

6. What are Hungary's two most important natural resources? Why are they important?

____

____

Extension: Choose a specific topic on the physical features of Hungary to research. Then share this information through your own travelogue that includes illustrations.

Name ______________________

History and Culture

1. In the box, draw and color the Hungarian flag with its correct colors.
2. List two important dates in Hungary's history and describe the events that took place on these dates.

____
____
____
____
____

3. Write the name of the first king of Hungary. Describe his rule.

____
____
____

4. In 1989, Hungary made major changes in its ______________ . How did this affect the country? ______________________

____
____

5. Define *spa*. How is this part of Hungary's culture? ______________________

____

6. List some other activities people in Hungary enjoy doing for recreation.

____

7. If you lived in Hungary, what would you do for recreation?

____

8. Pick one of Hungary's well-known composers. Write at least three facts about this person.

____
____
____

Source: ______________________ Page(s): ______________

Name ______________________

Physical Features

1. On the map, draw a star to mark the location of the capital of Iceland. Write the city's name next to the star.
2. Label the bodies of water that surround this island.
3. Label Iceland's largest glacier.
4. Why is Iceland called the "Land of Ice and Fire"?

    ____

    ____

    ____

    ____

5. Why is Iceland sometimes referred to as a land of "midnight sun"?

    ____

    ____

6. What is the only habitable area in Iceland? Why? ______________________

    ____

    ____

7. What is *Geysir*? ______________________

    ____

8. Describe the features of Iceland's inland plateau.

    ____

    ____

    ____

    ____

Extension: Prepare an oral report on one of the following topics that relates to Iceland: volcano, geyser, glacier, earthquake, or fault line.

Name ______________________

Physical Features

1. On the map, draw a star to show the location of Italy's capital. Write the city's name by the star.
2. Label the countries and the seas that border Italy.
3. What is the approximate length and width (at the widest point) of Italy?

   ____

   ____

4. List the six land regions of Italy excluding the islands.

   ____

   ____

   ____

   ____

   ____

   ____

   If you were able to go to only one of these regions, which one would it be and why?

   ____

   ____

5. Name the two island regions. ______________________
   Label them on the map.
6. Italy is shaped like what kind of footwear? ______________________
7. Describe Italy's climate. ______________________

   ____

8. Which mountain range attracts many skiers? ______________________

Extension: Choose one of the following topics to study: Alps, Apennine Tunnel, Arno River, Brenner Pass, Lake Como, Lake Maggiore, Matterhorn, Bay of Naples, Po River, Saint Bernard Passes, Tiber River, Tyrol, or Vesuvius. Take notes and write a report.

Name ____________________

History and Culture

1. Who designed the Italian flag?

   ____

   In the box, draw and color the flag.

2. Ancient Rome is very important in Italy's history. Explain why.

   ____

   ____

   ____

   ____

   ____

3. What is the basic unit of money in Italy? ____________________

4. Compare and contrast a popular way to travel in Venice to a popular way to travel in your area. ____________________

   ____

5. What is an *opera*? ____________________

   ____

   When and where were the first operas composed? ____________________

   ____

   Name four famous Italian composers. ____________________

   ____

6. Many famous artists were born and/or studied in Italy. Name at least six Italian artists.

   ____

   ____

   Choose one of these artists and write a short paragraph about that person, including the names of some of his works.

   ____

   ____

   ____

   ____

Name ____________________

Pictorial Map

Create a pictorial map of Italy. Draw 10 symbols that best represent the country. Complete the map key by listing your symbols and their meanings.

Name ____________________

Language

Use an encyclopedia, Italian dictionary, or another resource to help you complete these activities.

1. Write the correct numerals above the Italian number words. Give your source.

______ dieci	______ sei	______ due
______ otto	______ uno	______ nove
______ cinque	______ quattro	______ tre
______ sette	Source: ______	

2. In Italian, write the number words in the correct order. Add a comma between each number.

____

____

Food

Refer to an Italian cookbook and an encyclopedia for these activities.

1. How do Italian foods vary by region? Give examples.

____

____

____

2. On another sheet, draw and label 10 kinds of Italian pasta. Briefly explain the use of each.

Extension: Pretend that you are an Italian exchange student who wishes to prepare a special Italian meal for your American host family. Make a list of the dishes you will make and the ingredients you will need.

Name ____________________

Physical Features and General Information

1. On the map, draw a star to show the location of Latvia's capital. Write the city's name by the star.
2. Label the countries that border Latvia.
3. Label the Baltic Sea.
4. Draw and label the Western Dvina (Daugava) River.
5. In what year did Latvia gain its independence from the Soviet Union?

 ____

6. The official language of Latvia is ____________________.

 Latvia's language is related to what ancient Indian language? ____________________
7. What is the area of Latvia? ____________ sq. mi. ____________ sq. km.
8. What is another name for Latvians? ____________________ They make up what percent of the population? ____________ Name the other ethnic groups that make up Latvia's population. ____

 ____
9. What do Latvians do for recreation?

 ____

 ____

 ____

 ____
10. In the box, draw and color Latvia's flag.

Extension: Research religion in Latvia while the country was under Soviet control. Write two imaginary letters from a Latvian minister to his brother, one written before independence and one written after independence.

Name ______________________

Physical Features

1. On the map, draw a star to mark the location of the capital of Liechtenstein. Write the city's name by the star.
2. Draw and label the river that runs along the west border of Liechtenstein.
3. Use the symbol ^^^ to mark the highest region of Liechtenstein. What is the name and the elevation of the country's highest peak? ______________________
   ____
4. Color the country's strip of farmland green and the mountain areas brown.
5. What country borders Liechtenstein on the west? ______________________
   On the east? ______________________
   Label these countries on the map.
6. Liechtenstein's area is only ______________ sq. mi. or ______________ sq. km.
7. What type of animal is raised on the farms in Liechtenstein? ______________________
   What are the country's main manufactured products? ______________________
   ____
8. What type of climate would you find in Liechtenstein? ______________________
   What is the average temperature? ______________
   What is the average precipitation? ______________
   Compare the average temperature and precipitation in Liechtenstein to the temperature and precipitation in your area. Find the difference between each.
   ______________________ ______________________

Extension: Imagine taking a boat ride down the Rhine River. Where would you stop along your route? What would you see?

Name ______________________

History and Culture

1. In the box, draw and color the country's flag. Explain the meaning of the colors.

____

____

____

2. What was the last war in which Liechtenstein fought?

____

In what year did this occur? __________

3. Who has ruled the country since the early 1700s? ______________________

____

4. Tell what happened in Liechtenstein on each of these dates:

1719 ______________________

1815 ______________________

1866 ______________________

1868 ______________________

5. In what ways are Liechtenstein's close ties with the Swiss evident?

____

____

6. Briefly describe the lifestyle of the people of Liechtenstein. ______________________

____

____

7. What world-famous collection can be found in Vaduz? ______________________

Name some of the works that are a part of this collection. ______________________

____

In what way does the government use this collection? ______________________

____

8. What is the main religion of the people of Liechtenstein? ______________________

9. What is the official language of the country? ______________________

Name ____________________

Physical Features and General Information

1. On the map, draw a star to mark the location of the capital of Lithuania. Write the city's name by the star.
2. Use a dot to mark four other cities on the map. Write each name by the correct dot.
3. Label the countries that border Lithuania.
4. Briefly describe Lithuania's land.

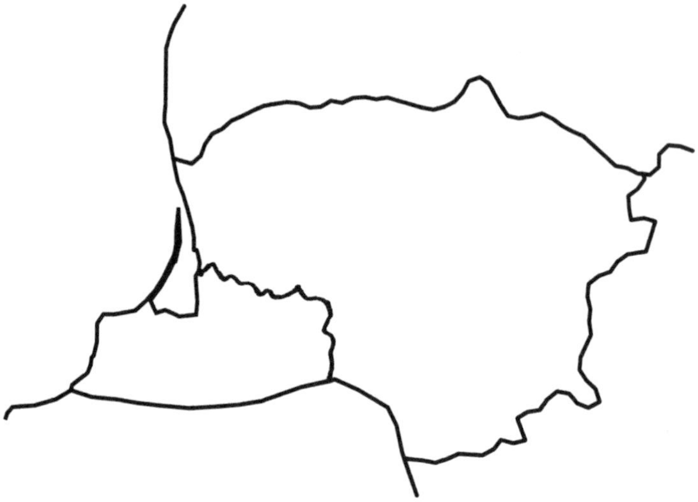

5. What were four changes that took place in Lithuania during Soviet rule?
6. In what year did Lithuania gain its independence from the Soviet Union? ____________
7. What are four of Lithuania's major industries? ____________
8. What is a *daino*? ____________
9. Describe a typical Lithuanian celebration. ____________
10. In the box, draw and color Lithuania's flag. Explain each color.

Name ____________________

Physical Features

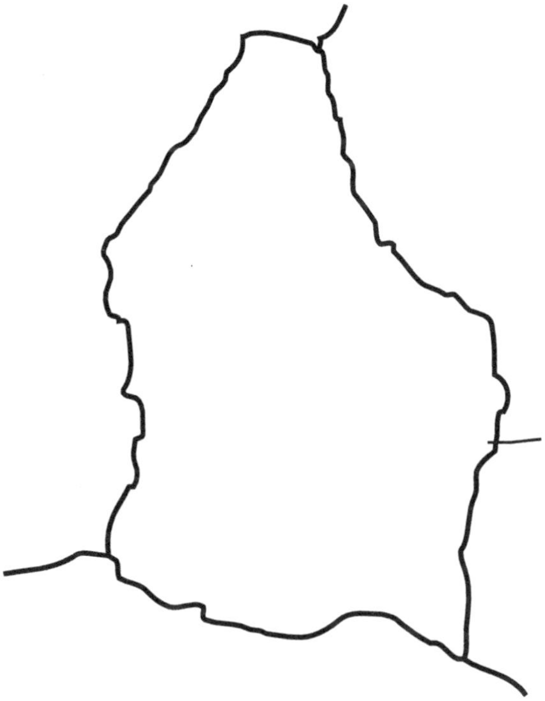

1. On the map, draw a star to mark the location of the capital of Luxembourg. Write the city's name by the star.
2. What is the population of the city of Luxembourg? ____________________
3. Draw and label the four rivers that run through Luxembourg.
4. Label the countries that border Luxembourg.
5. What is the highest point in Luxembourg?

   ____

   Mark this point with a **Λ** on the map.
6. What are the two main land regions of Luxembourg? Write a brief description of each region.

   ____

   ____

   ____

   ____
7. What is the most valuable resource of Luxembourg? ____________________
8. What are Luxembourg's chief exports? ____________________
9. What is the average temperature in Luxembourg in January? ____________________

   in July? ____________________ Compare Luxembourg's average temperatures to temperatures in your area. How much hotter/colder is it in these months in your area?

   ____

   ____

Extension: Trace a map of Luxembourg onto a blank sheet of paper. Trace a map of the smallest U.S. state on top of this map in a different color. The maps should be roughly the same scale. List the areas of both. Which is bigger?

Name ______________________

History and Culture

1. In the box, draw and color Luxembourg's flag. How were the colors of Luxembourg's flag chosen?

 ____

 ____

2. Who built the castle located on the site of the present-day city of Luxembourg?

 ____

 In what year was it built?____________
 In the A.D. 300s, who built the fort in what is now the city of Luxembourg?

 ____

3. Name four countries that have ruled Luxembourg. ______________________________

 ____

4. What World War II battle was fought in Luxembourg? When?______________________

 ____

5. The Luxembourgers are considered "prosperous" people. Explain.

 ____

 ____

 ____

6. What are the main occupations of the people of Luxembourg?____________________

 ____

7. What is the approximate population of Luxembourg? ______________________

8. What is the primary religion of the country? ______________________________

9. What are some of the favorite foods of the people of Luxembourg? ________________

 ____

10. Name the leading industry in Luxembourg. ______________________

Extension: Choose several dates in Luxembourg's history that you find interesting and make a historic time line.

Name ______________________

Language

1. What are the country's official languages? ______________________
   What is the everyday language of Luxembourg? ______________________
   What languages are taught in the schools? ______________________
2. Using a German dictionary or other resource, write the following words in German.
   river ______________ mountain ______________ forest ______________
   cattle ______________ grape ______________ castle ______________
3. Since French is also used in Luxembourg, write the same six words in French.
   river ______________ mountain ______________ forest ______________
   cattle ______________ grape ______________ castle ______________

Extension: Design a travel guide for a tourist visiting several Luxembourg cities. Include types of transportation, points of interest, and the miles between cities. Try to find pictures or illustrations for your guide. Include both German and French phrases that a tourist might use while visiting.

Name ____________________

Physical Features and General Information

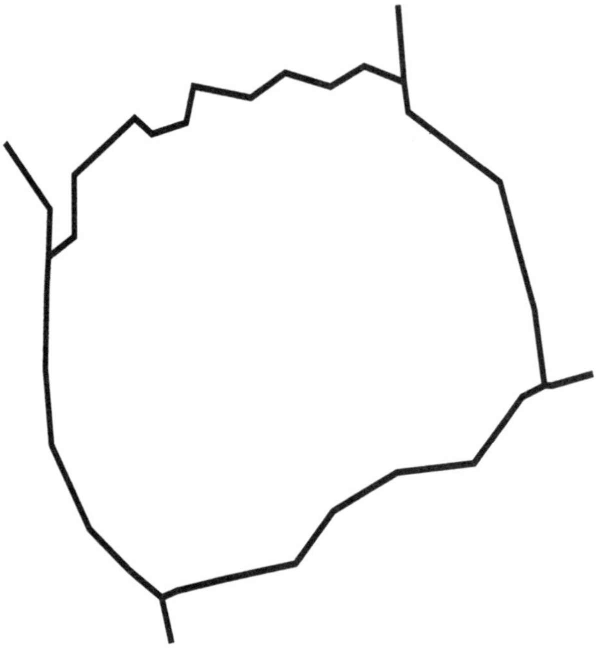

1. On the map, draw a star to mark the location of the capital of Macedonia. Write the city's name by the star.
2. Label the countries that border Macedonia.
3. Macedonia's landscape is filled with

   ____________________ .

   Most of the country lies on a plateau that is how many feet above sea level?

   ____
4. List the name and height of Macedonia's highest point. Label it on the map.

   ____

   ____
5. Describe Macedonia's climate. ____________________

   ____
6. Macedonia's official language is ____________________ .
7. List four of Macedonia's ethnic groups. ____________________

   Which one is the majority? ____________________
8. Macedonia was part of ____________________ from 1945 to 1990. In 1990, the ____________________ lost control of the government and Macedonia declared its independence. However, many nations refused to recognize it as an ____________________ ____________________ .
9. What percentage of all Macedonians live in cities? ____________________
10. Macedonian music shows influence from the ____________________ who ruled the region between which centuries? ____________________
11. What is the *oro*? ____________________
12. Why did/does Greece have a problem with Macedonia's name and status as a country?

    ____

    ____

Name ______________________

Physical Features

1. On the map, draw a star to mark the location of Malta's capital. Write the city's name by the star.

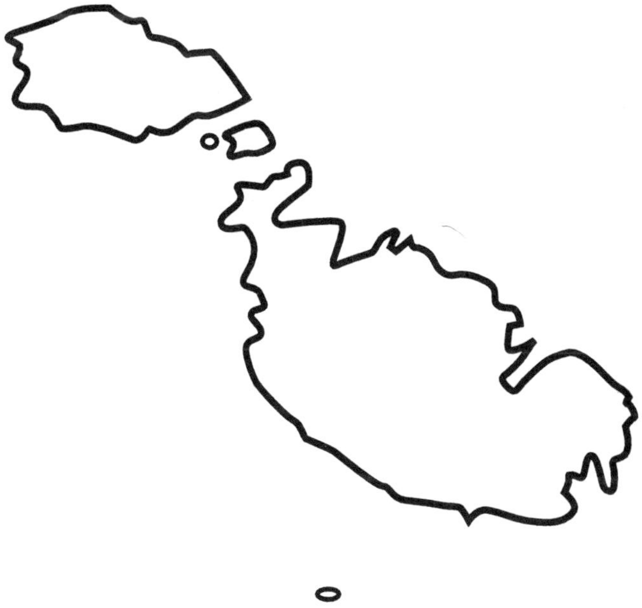

2. Malta is an island country. Name the five islands that make up this country.

3. Which of these islands are uninhabited?

4. Label the body of water that surrounds Malta.
5. Read about the climate, average temperature, and rainfall in Malta. How is it similar or different from the area where you live? ______________________
6. What is terrace farming? Why do you think this type of farming is used in Malta?

Extension: In the box, draw a diagram of a terrace farm.

Name ______________________

History and Culture

1. In the box, draw and color the Maltese flag. Explain the meaning of the insignia on the flag.

____

____

2. What is the Maltese national anthem?

____

3. Why was Malta of such great military significance in wartime?

____

____

____

4. Describe the role Malta played in World War II. ______________________

____

5. What nation was the last to own Malta? ______________________

When did Malta become an independent country? ______________________

6. About one-third of the Maltese people work in the dockyards. Why is this such an important business? ______________________

____

7. What ancient relics have been found in Malta? ______________________

____

____

8. How does Malta's school system compare with your country's? ______________________

____

____

____

Extension: Write a short story that takes place during World War II in Malta's underground passages.

Name ______________________

Language and Food

1. What are the official languages of Malta? ______________________
2. Why do you think the country of Malta, located between Italy and Africa, has English newspapers? ______________________
3. What are some of the crops grown in Malta? ______________________
4. Why must the people of Malta import most of their food? ______________________

   What are the three main countries that export food products to Malta? ______________________

   What types of foods are imported? ______________________
5. Find a recipe that might be used by the Maltese. Base your choice on Malta's location and the types of crops and animals grown or raised on their farms.

   Recipe: ______________________ Source: ______________________

   Ingredients: ______________________

   Preparation: ______________________
6. Name the countries that most likely influence Maltese cuisine. ______________________

Name ______________________

Physical Features/General Information

1. On the map, draw a star to mark the location of Moldova's capital city. Write the name by the star.

2. Moldova is sandwiched between which two countries? Label these countries on the map.

 ____

 ____

3. Moldova's land could be described as

 ______________________________ .

4. Moldova has over ____________________ rivers, the main one being the

 ______________________________ .

 Draw and label it on the map.

5. Before belonging to the Soviet Union, Moldova belonged to what country? ______________

6. Like many other former Soviet-ruled countries, Moldova declared its independence in what year? ____________

7. What is Moldova's official language? ______________________________

8. Why do you think Moldova's parliament ordered the Cyrillic (Russian) alphabet to be replaced by the Roman alphabet?

 ____

 ____

 ____

9. Provide details about Moldova's population such as its density and distribution.

 ____

 ____

 In what occupation do most of the population work? ______________________

Extension: Research to find the Cyrillic alphabet. Write a short message using this alphabet.

Name ______________________

Physical Features and General Information

1. On the map, draw a star to mark the location of Monaco's capital city. Write the city's name by the star.
2. What country borders Monaco on three sides?

   ____

   What borders Monaco on its remaining side? ______________________

3. Write the names of the four distinct parts of Monaco where they are located on the map.
4. What makes Monaco an important tourist resort?

   ____

   ____

   ____

5. Compare Monaco's size, in area, to the smallest U.S. state.

   ____

   ____

6. The principal language of Monaco is ______________________ .

   Most natives speak a dialect called ______________________ , which is related to ______________ and ______________ .

7. Colorful postage stamps are important to Monaco's economy. Design one for them illustrating one of their well-known attractions.

Extension: Find brochures, travel posters, or other tourist information on Monaco. Display these in your classroom. Also, design and display a tourist map of Monaco showing these places: Cathedral of Monaco, Government Palace, Grand Theatre, Marine Museum, Museum of Fine Arts, Museum of Prehistoric Anthropology.

Name ______________________

History and Culture

1. In the box, draw and color Monaco's flag with its correct colors.
2. What is Monaco's type of government?

   ____

   Explain briefly how this type of government works.

   ____

   ____

   ____
3. What important changes came when Monaco's constitution was revised in 1962?

   ____

   ____
4. What countries have ruled Monaco from 700 B.C. to the present? ______________________

   ____
5. Why has Monaco reclaimed land from the sea? ______________________

   ____
6. What effect do you think the French had on the cultural development of the people of Monaco? ______________________

   ____
7. What are natives of Monaco called? ______________________
8. Why have many people of other countries located to Monaco? ______________________

   ____
9. What is unique about the Princess Caroline Library? ______________________

   ____

Extension: Pretend that you are a tour guide for the country of Monaco. Write a brief presentation to give your tourists as you travel from the Casino dEté down Princess Grace Avenue to the Palace of the Prince. Include information about Prince Rainier, Prince Albert, Princess Grace, and Princess Caroline.

Name ____________________

Physical Features

1. On the map, draw two stars: one blue star to show the location of the capital of the Netherlands and one red star to show the seat of government. Print the city names by each star.
2. Label the countries and the sea that border the Netherlands.
3. Divide the map into its four main land regions. Color each region a different color. Set up a map key to show what region each color represents.
4. Two-fifths of the Netherlands was once covered with water. The people created polders to make this land usable. Explain *polders* and how they were created.

____
____
____
____
____
____

5. What purposes do the canals serve? ____________________
____
6. What region has the most productive farmland and the country's largest cities?
____
7. Briefly describe the country's climate. ____________________
____
____

Extension: Find information about the catastrophe in the delta area in 1953. Take notes and share this information with your classmates.

Name ______________________

History and Culture

1. In the box, draw and color the flag. How did the flag change after 1630?

   ____

   ____

2. Who controlled the Netherlands from 1516 to 1648?

   ____

3. Why were the 1600s called the "Golden Age of the Netherlands"?

   ____

   ____

   ____

4. Tell what important event involving the United States took place in 1624.

   ____

   ____

5. How did the Netherlands recover after the devastation of World War II?

   ____

   ____

6. What are the main occupations of the Dutch? ______________________

   ____

7. How is the Netherlands's high school educational system different from that in your country?

   ____

   ____

   ____

8. Name several of the Netherlands's great painters. If possible, find illustrations of their works to show in class.

   ____

   ____

Extension: Find a story or poem that tells about the dikes or canals of the Netherlands. Discuss with others why dikes and canals make interesting material for stories and poetry.

Name ______________________

Language

1. The Dutch language is part of what language group? ______________________
2. Use a dictionary, encyclopedia, or resource person to define these words:

   kermis ______________________ Netherlands ______________________

   klompen ______________________ Sinterklaas ______________________

   gezelligheid ______________________ yacht ______________________
3. Write several Dutch words that represent objects in the Netherlands. Give their English translations. Name the source where you found the information.

   ____

   ____
4. What is the IJsselmeer? ______________________

The Hague

1. Write three sentences that describe or tell about The Hague.

   ____

   ____

   ____

   ____

   ____

   ____
2. Who contributed the funds to build The Hague's Peace Palace? ______________________

   Why was the Peace Palace built? ______________________

   ____

   ____

   ____

Name ____________________

Physical Features and General Information

1. On the map, draw a star to mark the location of Norway's capital city. Write the capital's name by the star.
2. Label the Sogne Fiord.
3. Label the countries and the ocean that border Norway.
4. Use a ∧ to mark Norway's tallest mountain on the map. Label it.
5. Draw and label the Glåma River.
6. The full length of Norway's coastline is 13,267 miles. How does this compare to the distance around the world?

   ____
   ____
   ____

7. What is a *fiord*? ____________________

   ____

8. Name the two largest island groups off the Norway coast.

   ____________________ ____________________

9. When and why did mining become an important economic activity in Norway?

   ____

10. How does the social welfare system benefit Norway's people? ____________________

    ____

11. Where is Lapland? Describe the clothing and housing of those who live there.

    ____
    ____
    ____

Extension: Write a brief summary giving reasons for the mild climate along the western coast of Norway in winter and its cooler climate in summer.

Name ______________________

History and Culture

1. In the box, draw and color the flag.
2. How long ago were people living in Norway? ______________________
3. List three facts about the Viking period.

____
____
____
____
____

4. How do the physical features of Norway affect the lifestyle of its people? ______________________
____
5. What three Norwegian writers have won the Nobel Prize for Literature? ______________________
____

   Choose one of these writers and give the year and the name of the literary work that won the Nobel Prize.

   ____
6. Tell what style of music Edvard Grieg composed. List a few of his compositions by title.
____
____
7. Explain how the educational system of Norway differs from the system in your country.
____
____
8. Who was Henrik Ibsen? ______________________ Why was he called the father of modern drama? ______________________

   List some of his works. ______________________

Extension: Choose an event that greatly affected the economy of Norway. Share this information with your classmates. How would the country be different if this event had not happened or if it had had a different outcome?

Name ____________________

Physical Features and Government

1. On the map, draw a star to identify the location of the capital city of Poland. Write the capital's name by the star.
2. Name Poland's seven land areas.

   ____
   ____
   ____
   ____
   ____
   ____
   ____

3. Which of these areas would you choose to live in? Why?

   ____
   ____
   ____

4. On the map, draw and label these rivers: Vistula, Bug, Oder, and Warta.
5. Label the sea and the countries that border Poland.
6. What is Poland's most important natural resource? ____________________
7. Calculate the number of miles from New York City to Warsaw, Poland. ____________________
8. Poland is one of the world's leading producers of what two products?

   ____

9. Poland's parliament is called ____________________. It is made up of two houses; The lower house, or ____________________, and the upper house, or ____________________.
10. Who presently heads the Polish government? ____________________
11. When was the first time free elections were held in Poland since the 1940s? ____________________

Extension: Read about Lech Walesa. Share this information in a report or story.

Name ____________________

History and Culture

1. In the box, draw and correctly color the flag of Poland.
2. What is the national anthem and what does it mean?

____
____
____
____

3. When did Poland become an independent republic? ____________
4. Name four significant events in Poland's history that affected its world position.

____
____
____
____

5. Explain how labor strikes in the 1980s affected Poland's work environment.

____
____

6. What recreational activities are popular in Poland? ____________________
7. In what major way has the Poles' lifestyle changed since 1900? ____________________

____

8. Why is the standard of living lower in Poland than in Western European countries?

____

9. What famous composer wrote music based on Polish dances? ____________________
10. Name three Poles who have won the Nobel Prize. ____________________

____

Extension: Draw maps showing the partitioning that occurred in Poland in 1918, in 1939, and in 1945.

Name ____________________

Physical Features

1. On the map, draw a star to identify the location of Portugal's capital city. Write the city's name by the star.
2. Label the country and body of water that border Portugal.
3. Name Portugal's four main land regions.
4. What is the *meseta*?
5. On the map, draw and label the three major rivers of Portugal.
6. Name at least three of Portugal's natural resources.
7. Use a ∧ to mark Portugal's highest point on the map. Name this point and give its elevation. ____________________
8. On the map, draw a dot to mark the second largest Portuguese city. Write its name by the dot.
9. Where do the majority of Portugal's people live? ____________________
10. Compare and contrast the lifestyles of the residents of Porto or Lisbon with a small town or village in Portugal.

Extension: Describe a typical Portuguese farm. Compare it to a typical large midwestern U.S. farm.

Name ______________________

History and Culture

1. In the box, draw and correctly color the flag. What do its colors signify?

____

____

____

____

2. What is the national anthem?

____

3. What were the first Portuguese inhabitants called? ______________________________

4. Name three Portuguese explorers of the 1400s and 1500s. ______________________________

____

Pick one and tell about his voyage.

____

____

5. What are four favorite Portuguese recreational activities? ______________________________

____

6. How do Portuguese bullfights differ from those of Spain and Latin America? ______________

____

7. Portuguese architects used ornate designs called *Manueline* in buildings. Give an example of this art form and note for whom it was named.

____

____

8. Name the most famous literary work of Portugal's golden age. ______________________________

Who wrote this epic poem? ______________________________

Tell briefly the main theme of the poem. ______________________________

____

Extension: Pretend you were a crewmember for one of the famous Portuguese explorers. Write a journal entry that illustrates your part in an exploration.

Name ______________________

Language

1. What is the official language of Portugal? ______________________

   It is often referred to as one of the romance languages. Tell why. ______________________

   ____
2. What is the basic unit of money in Portugal? ______________________
3. How many principal Portuguese dialects are there? ______________________
4. How did the language change after 1943? ______________________

   ____
5. How did Portugal get its name? ______________________

   ____
6. Tell how these three words relate to music: *chulas, viras, fados.*

   ____

   ____

   ____

Miracle of Fátima

1. Where in Portugal is the village of Fátima located? ______________________
2. What important event reportedly occurred there in 1917? ______________________

   ____

   ____

   How did this affect the future of Fátima? ______________________

   ____
3. Read about the miracle at Fátima. List important details about this story.

   ____

   ____

   ____

   ____

Name ____________________

Physical Features

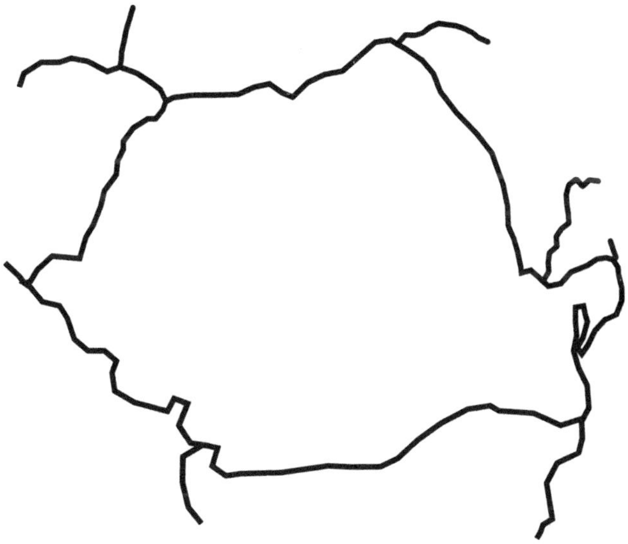

1. On the map, draw a star to mark the location of Romania's capital city. Write the city's name by the star.
2. Using a red pencil, marker, or pen, draw in the six land regions of Romania and label them.
3. Draw the Danube River using a blue pen or pencil.
4. Label the countries and body of water that border Romania.
5. Is Romania larger or smaller in size than the state or province where you live? By how much?

   ____

6. List four of Romania's natural resources.

   ____

7. Imagine you are vacationing in Romania and traveling through each of its six regions. Write about your travels and include details about each of the regions. Use the back of this page, if necessary.

   ____

Name ______________________

History and Culture

1. In the box, draw and color Romania's flag in the correct colors.
2. How did Romania get its name?

   ____

   ____

3. With whom did Romania join forces during World War I?

   ____

   ____

4. Romania was a Soviet satellite. Define *Soviet satellite*. ______________________

   ____

5. What is another spelling of Romania? ______________________
6. Who are Gypsies? ______________________________

   ____

7. Look up *Dracula*. In what region of Romania does this story take place? __________

   ____

8. What are some differences between a state farm and a collective farm?

   ____

   ____

   ____

   ____

   How are Romanian farms changing? ______________________

   ____

9. Why is the Romanian language unique? ______________________

   ____

10. Rural Romanians decorate their cottages using ______________________

    ____.

Extension: Research Nicolae Ceausescu. Write a mock newspaper account of his last days in Romania.

Name ____________________

Physical Features

1. On the map, draw a star to show the location of Russia's capital city. Write its name by the star.
2. Label the following on the map above.

Caspian Sea	Ob River	Kara Sea
Black Sea	Volga River	Arctic Ocean
Barents Sea	Lena River	Bering Sea
Lake Baikal	Yenisey River	Sea of Okhotsk
Ural Mountains	all the bordering countries	

3. What is permafrost? How much of this country is covered by it?

____

4. Where does most of this region's rainfall occur? ____________________

____

5. List four of Russia's natural resources.

____________________ ____________________

____________________ ____________________

6. What boundary do the Ural Mountains form? ____________________

____

7. On another sheet, describe either Russia's four zones or its five land regions.

Extension: Plan a trip to Russia. Outline your journey in pencil on the map above and tell a few interesting facts about four of the places you visited.

Name ____________________

General Information

1. What is Russia's basic unit of money? ____________________
2. Do 75 percent of Russia's people live in urban or rural areas? ____________________
3. Why is there a severe housing shortage in Russian cities?

____

____

____

4. Describe the problems many people have living in Moscow.

____

____

____

____

____

5. The country's official language, ____________________, is written in the ____________________ alphabet.
6. Research the Russian alphabet and copy it here.

7. What are some popular Russian dishes? ____________________

____

____

8. Define *sovkhozy* and *kolkhozy*. ____________________

____

____

Extension: Research Catherine the Great. Pretend first that you were a famous Russian composer and second that you were a poor serf. Describe what life would have been like under Catherine's rule for each of these two people.

Name ____________________

History and Culture

1. In the box, draw and correctly color the flag.
2. What happened to the Soviet Union in 1991? How did this affect Russia?

 ____

 ____

 ____

 ____

3. What is a czar? ____________________

 ____

4. Who was Ivan the Terrible? ____________________

 Describe him. ____________________

 ____

 ____

5. What Russians have won the Nobel Prize for literature? List one title of a famous work written by each.

 ____

 ____

 ____

6. Who was Tchaikovsky? ____________________

 ____

 List two of his works. ____________________

7. For many centuries, Russian artists produced icons. What is an *icon*? ____________________

 ____

8. Name two famous Russian ballet companies.

 ____

9. Russia is known for what type of architecture? ____________________

Extension: Choose an event, movement, or important figure from Russia's past to research and study. Share this information with your class in the form of a report, play, story, art activity, or project of your choice.

Name ______________________

Physical Features

1. On the map, draw a star to mark the location of the capital city of San Marino. Write the city's name by the star.
2. What country surrounds San Marino?

   ____

3. On what mountain does San Marino lie? ______________________

   Draw a ∧ to mark the highest peak. Label it.
4. What structure surrounds the city of San Marino?

   ____

   ____

5. What parts of the capital city's wall are symbols of the country?______________________

   ____

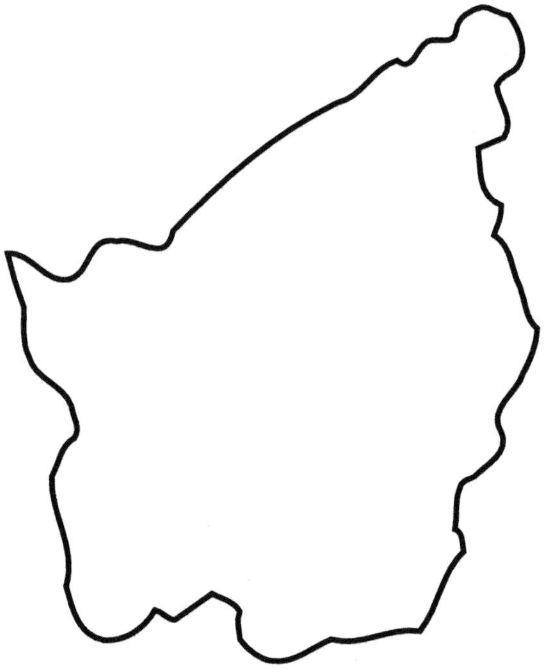

6. Is San Marino the oldest or newest republic in the world? ______________________
7. What is San Marino's total area? ______________________
8. What is its approximate population? ______________________
9. What do San Marino's people have in common with the people of northern Italy?

   ____

10. Describe the occupations of most San Marino people. ______________________

    ____

11. What makes San Marino an attractive place to visit? ______________________

    ____

Extension: San Marino is known for its beautiful postage stamps. After reading about its culture, design a new stamp for it.

Name ____________________

Physical Features and General Information

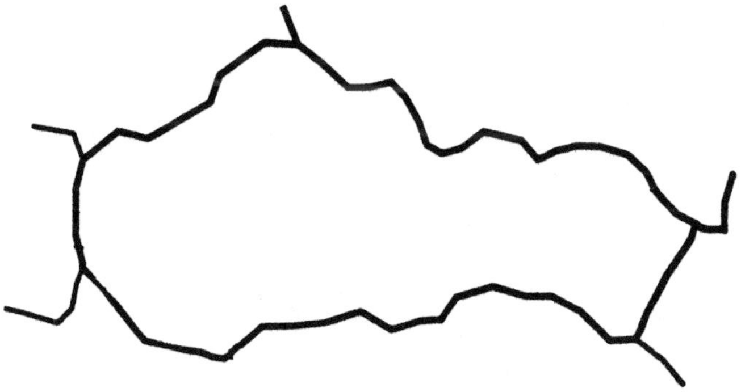

1. On the map, draw a star to identify the location of the capital city of Slovakia. Write its name by the star.
2. Label the five countries that border Slovakia.
3. What are the three major mountain ranges in Slovakia?

   ____

   ____

   ____
4. Why was the former Czechoslovakia split into Slovakia and the Czech Republic?

   ____

   ____

   ____
5. What happened in 1989 and how did it affect the former Czechoslovakia?

   ____

   ____

   ____
6. Name the population groups found in Slovakia.

   ____

   Who forms Slovakia's largest minority? ____________________
7. Is the Slovakian standard of living higher or lower than most former Communist European countries? ____________________
8. What do many city families own? ____________________

Extension: Pretend that tension exists among the ethnic groups living in your neighborhood in Slovakia. To foster good will, your family has decided to host a party at which each family brings an ethnic dish. List on another sheet the three ethnic groups along with the dish they might bring. Give the recipe for each dish.

Name ______________________

Physical Features and General Information

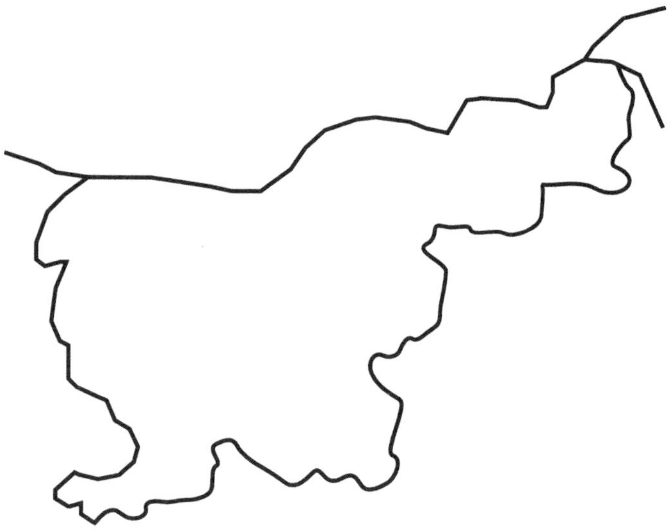

1. On the map, draw a star to show the location of Slovenia's capital. Write its name by the star.
2. Label the countries that border Slovenia.
3. What type of landform covers most of the country? ______________________
4. Label the Julian Alps with ʌʌʌ. What is the name and height of the country's highest point?

   ____

   ______________ feet

   ______________ meters
5. What is the *Karst*? ______________________

   ____
6. What is the country's official language? ______________________
7. Slovenia was once part of ______________________, but declared its independence in 1991.
8. Slovenia's major group of people are called ______________________.
9. Who is considered the father of Slovenian literature? ______________________

   For what is he known? ______________________

   ____
10. In what two areas are most Slovenians employed?

    ____
11. If you visited Slovenia, what would you like to see? ______________________

    ____

    ____

Extension: Research Slovenia's *Kurenti* festival. Design and make a construction paper animal mask to be used at a *Kurenti* festival.

Name ______________________

age

ish-English dictionary or encyclopedia to complete the activities below.

e Spanish words for the numerals one through ten.

______ ______ ______ ______

______ ______ ______ ______

______ ______

meanings of the following Spanish words:

bueno	madre	gato
______	______	______
gazpacho	escuela	casa
______	______	______

or three advertisements or an article written in Spanish. On another sheet, note t the words that are similar in both languages. Then have these translated by a peaking person.

l foods or drinks we consume that originated in Spain. Use a Spanish cookbook or if necessary.

______ ______ ______ ______

______ ______ ______ ______

food a staple food in Spain? ______________________

____

e for *paella*. Write it on a card to share with others.

e do urban-dwelling Spanish eat the evening meal? ______________________

ties do they often do before and after the meal? ______________________

____

a class or family project, plan a meal including only Spanish cuisine. Credit your rce for recipes and food ideas.

Name ______________________

Physical Features and General Information

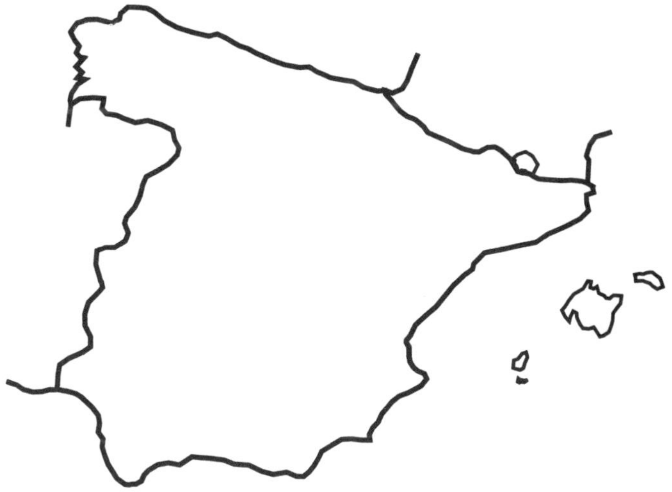

1. On the map, draw a star to mark the location of Spain's capital city. Write the city's name by the star.
2. Label the three countries and the sea and ocean that border Spain.
3. On the map, draw the boundaries of the seven major land regions and label each one.
4. What is Spain's area in square miles and square kilometers?

   ______________ sq. miles

   ______________ sq. kilometers
5. On the map, draw and label Spain's two longest rivers.
6. Mark the second largest city with a dot and then write its name.
7. What is Spain's most important natural resource? ______________
8. Research the Canary Islands. How did they get their name? ______________

   ____
9. List three facts about the Balearic Islands. Give your source.

   ____

   ____

   ____

   ______________________ Page(s): ______

   Source(s): ______________________
10. What natural boundary separates Spain and France? ______________

Extension: Plan a trip to Spain. Since it is such a large country, you have time to visit only four places. Trace your route on a copy of a map of Spain. Below the map, list and describe your stops. On the map, write the number of miles between consecutive points on your journey. Tell why these places were chosen.

Name ____________

History

1. In the box, draw and color Spain's flag with its correct colors.
2. What is the national anthem? ____________
3. What famous non-Spanish explorer started a great age of exploration and conquest for Spain? ____________

   When did he do this? ____________
4. Name two other explorers of this time and list one accomplishment for each. ____________
5. What was the Spanish Inquisition? ____________
6. What caused Spain to lose the empire it had acquired in the 1500s? ____________
7. What was the Spanish Armada? What happened to it in 1588? ____________
8. What kind of ruler was Francisco Franco? How long did he rule? ____________
9. When did Spain begin to establish a democracy? ____________

Extension: Read about Spain's role in the American Revolutionary War. Write a letter, detailing Spain's war strategy, from an imaginary Spanish general to George Washington.

Name ____________

Culture

1. Why can ancient Roman ruins be found in parts of Spain? ____________
2. Describe a typical Spanish workday for city workers. ____________
3. What is a *paseo*? How does it fit in with the Spanish lifestyle? ____________
4. How does life in the country differ from that of the city? ____________
5. Name two important sporting events in Spain. ____________
6. Spain is rich in artistic traditions. Name several famous artist ____________

   Choose one artist on which to research and report.
7. Miguel de Cervantes, a Spanish author, wrote what literary n

   What is the main theme of this literary work? ____________
8. Read about the music of Spain. Name three world-famous Sp ____________

   Find tapes or recordings of the type of music that accompani with classmates.

Extension: Read about Madrid and Barcelona. As an art proje these two cities. Include places of interest, historic various kinds of recreation and entertainment. Tr your brochure. Include illustrations.

Langu

Use a Span

1. Write th
2. Give the

   siesta

   mucho
3. Find two and repor Spanish-s

Food

1. List sever dictionary
2. Why is sea
3. Find a reci
4. At what tir

   What activ

Extension: As so

Name ______________________

Physical Features

1. On the map, draw a star to mark the location of Sweden's capital city. Write the city's name by the star.
2. Mark with a ● and label three other large cities.
3. Label the countries and the sea and gulf that border Sweden.
4. Name and briefly describe Sweden's four main land regions.

____
____
____
____
____
____
____
____

5. Draw and label on the map the two largest lakes in Sweden.
6. What are Sweden's most important natural resources? ______________________________________
____
7. How does Sweden compare in area to the other European countries?
____
8. How does its population compare? ______________________________________
9. Research both Sweden's climate and its recreational activities. Tell what time of year you would choose to visit, where you would go, and what activities you would do once there.
____
____
____
10. Sweden is considered a Scandinavian country along with which of its neighbors?
____

Name ____________________

History

1. In the box, draw and correctly color Sweden's flag. When was it first used?

____

2. What is the national anthem?

____

____

____

3. Where did the Swedish Vikings explore?

____

____

4. In early history, what countries made up the Union of Kalmar?

____

5. Who was Gustavus Vasa? What did he do? ____________________

____

____

6. Research types of Swedish occupations from the early 1800s to the present. Then write short descriptions of workers from three different time periods. For each worker, include the time period, a made-up Swedish name, his/her occupation, and what work conditions were like.

____

____

____

____

____

____

____

____

7. What chemical explosive was invented by Alfred Nobel? ____________________

When was it patented? ____________________

Extension: Research important dates in Sweden's history. On a separate sheet of paper, give the dates and historical events that also involved Norway and Denmark.

Name ____________________

Culture

1. Sweden has one of the highest standards of living in the world. Give several reasons why this is true.

____

____

2. What is the basic unit of money in Sweden? ____________________
3. What are Sweden's chief winter sports? ____________________
4. Describe the Vasa Race. ____________________

____

5. Who was the first Swedish writer to win the Nobel Prize? ____________________

What children's book did she write? ____________________

If possible, locate this book and share it with your class.

6. List several ways in which the Lapps who live in Sweden's far north differ from most other Swedes. ____________________

____

7. What is *smörgasbord*? ____________________

____

Draw two smörgasbords below, one depicting Swedish foods and one showing your favorites.

Extension: Research Swedish holidays. Write reports on St. Lucia Day and Midsummer's Eve. Include illustrations.

Name ______________________

Physical Features

1. On the map, draw a star to mark the location of Switzerland's capital city. Write its name by the star.
2. Mark the cities of Geneva and Zurich with a heavy dot. Write each name by the correct dot.
3. Label the countries that border Switzerland.
4. What are the three main land regions of Switzerland?

   ____

   ____

   ____

5. Draw and label the Rhine River, the Rhône River, the Inn River, and the Ticino River.
6. Draw Lake Constance and Lake Geneva. Color Lake Constance blue and label Lake Geneva.
7. What is Switzerland's greatest natural resource? How does this resource benefit Switzerland?

   ____

   ____

8. What causes the wide variety of temperatures in Switzerland? ______________________
   Make a bar graph or a chart showing temperature variations in the Alps compared with the Swiss Plateau.
9. Research the Matterhorn. On the back of this page, write a comparison in location, elevation, and general area topography with Mt. McKinley in the U.S.
10. Bicycling, target shooting, and bobsledding are three popular Swiss activities. Tell where in the country and during what time of year you would do each one.

    bicycling: ______________________

    target shooting: ______________________

    bobsledding: ______________________

Extension: Research the Swiss Alps. Write a report giving important facts that visitors and tourists would like to know. Create a three-dimensional design of a mountain resort in the Alps.

Name ______________________

History

1. In the box, draw and color Switzerland's flag. What does the cross represent?

   ____

2. List five groups of people who occupied what is now Switzerland between 100 B.C. and A.D. 800.

   ____

   ____

   ____

   ____

   ____

3. What is Switzerland's unit of money? ______________________ Give two reasons why people all over the world do their banking in Switzerland. ______________________

   ____

4. What was the Perpetual Covenant? ______________________

   ____

5. What world-renowned organization was founded in 1863 by Jean Henri Dunant?

   ____

6. When did Switzerland first establish a policy of neutrality? ____________

7. Give several reasons why Switzerland was able to maintain neutrality throughout World War I and World War II. ______________________

   ____

8. Do you agree with Switzerland's policy of neutrality? Why, or why not?

   ____

   ____

   ____

Extension: Research John Calvin. Write a paragraph from an imaginary diary he might have kept in Geneva in 1538.

Name ____________________

Culture

1. What special types of music are unique to Switzerland? ____________________

   ____

   Find tapes or records of Swiss music to bring to the class and play.

2. Draw an alphorn. Explain its construction. What is it used for?

   ____

   ____

   ____

3. Would you say music plays an important part in the life of the Swiss? Why?

   ____

   ____

   ____

4. What are two well-known Swiss children's classics? Who are the authors?

   ____

   ____

5. What is *hornussen*? ____________________

   ____

6. Switzerland is a thriving industrial nation. Name three important goods they manufacture.

   ____

   ____

7. What is *Dadaism*? ____________________

   ____

8. In what area do most of the Swiss people live? ____________________

   Draw a picture of a Swiss chalet on another sheet.

Extension: Swiss watchmaking is world famous. Research this topic. You may wish to consult a local jeweler. Write several reasons why watchmaking is important to the Swiss people.

Name ______________________

Language

1. What are the official languages of Switzerland? ______________________

____

2. Write the word "Switzerland" in the official languages of the country.

______________ ______________ ______________

3. What are the national languages? ______________________

4. Define these words:

Helvitia ______________________

Landsgemeinde ______________________

Schwyzerdütsch ______________________

Emmentaler ______________________

5. Write 10 words you think a tourist might need to know while touring Switzerland. Since three languages are spoken—French, German, and Italian—write the words in all three languages. Give your sources.

English	**French**	**German**	**Italian**

Sources: ______________________

____

Name ____________________

Physical Features

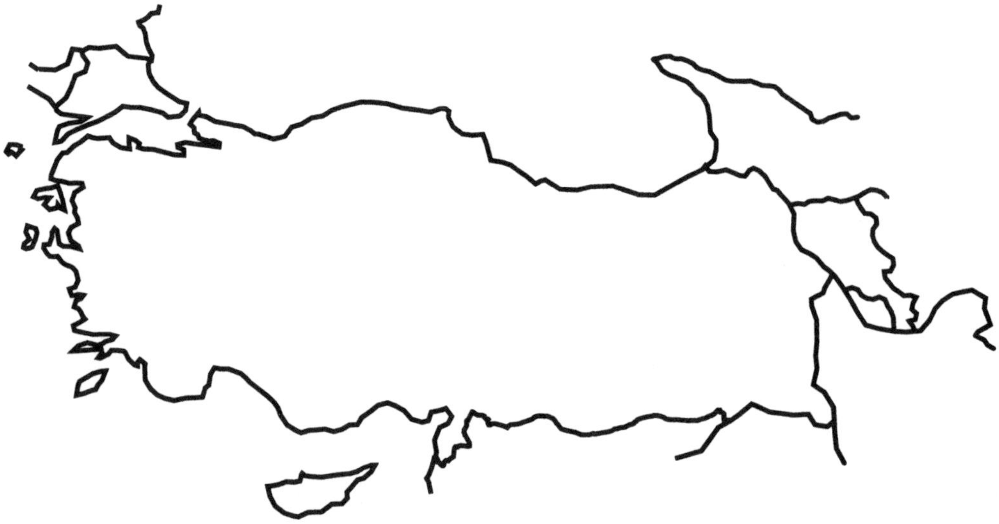

1. On the map, draw a star to show the location of Turkey's capital. Write the city's name by the star.
2. Turkey is located on which two continents? ____________________
3. Name the part of Turkey that is in Europe. ____________________
4. On the map, label the two major seas and the countries that border Turkey.
5. Label the Bosporous, the Sea of Marmara, and the Dardanelles. What are these three bodies of water called? ____________________ Describe their importance to Turkey.

   ____

   ____

6. Research Istanbul. Tell why its location is unique and describe old and new sections.

   ____

   ____

   ____

7. What are Turkey's eight major land regions?

   ____

   ____

   Study one land region or feature thoroughly. Present an oral report on that region or physical feature.

Name ____________________

History and Culture

1. In the box, draw and correctly color the Turkish flag.
2. What was the Ottoman Empire? Why was it later called "the Sick Man of Europe"?

____

____

____

____

3. Istanbul was once known as ____________________, the city of Constantine. Constantine I, emperor of ____________________ made it his capital. The Greeks before him called it ____________________.
4. Describe two types of Turkish houses. On the back of this sheet, draw and label these two types of houses.

____

____

5. Name and describe three Turkish foods. Draw an asterisk (*) by any you have eaten.

____

____

____

____

6. Turkey's most important contribution to the arts is fine architecture. Name at least two famous buildings found in Istanbul.

____

7. If you visited Turkey for a week, what would you like to see, taste, touch, smell, and hear?

____

____

____

8. Study the famous rugs designed in Turkey. Then design your own Turkish rug.

Name ____________________

Physical Features

1. On the map, draw a star to show the location of Ukraine's capital. Write its name by the star.
2. Label the countries and the waters that border Ukraine.
3. List the six major land regions of Ukraine.

____
____
____
____
____
____

4. What are *steppes*? Why are they important in Ukraine's economy?

____
____

5. Describe the Central Plateau. What seemingly opposite economic activities make it a valuable region? ____________________

____
____

6. Europe's third longest river, the ____________________, runs through northern Ukraine to what sea? ____________________ Draw and label this river on the map.
7. Describe Ukraine's climate. ____________________

____

8. Why is Ukraine known as the "breadbasket of Europe"?

____
____

Extension: Research farming in the Ukraine. Choose two items you would raise for one year on a new, private farm in Ukraine. After learning about how to raise your crops/livestock, create a month-by-month plan showing what would have to be done each month of the year.

Name ______________________

History and Culture

1. In the box, draw and correctly color the flag. When was it adopted? __________
   What do its stripes symbolize?
   ____
   ____
   ____
2. After a brief period of independence in 1918, Ukraine became subject to rule by what was initially called
   ______________________________________ . Later it became part of the
   ____________________________ .
3. When did it gain its recent independence? __________
4. What is now the official language? ________________________
5. What are Ukraine's two largest ethnic groups? ____________________________
6. What was *Russification*? ____
   ____
7. What is Ukraine's official policy toward language used by minority ethnic groups?
   ____
   ____
8. What are *pysanky*? ____
   ____
9. Define *bandura* and *hopak*.
   ____
   ____

Extension: Research the city of Odessa. What Olympic gold medalist figure skater is from this city? Describe what her life might have been like as a child growing up in Ukraine.

Name ______________________

Physical Features and General Information

1. When did Vatican City become the smallest independent state in the world?

   ____

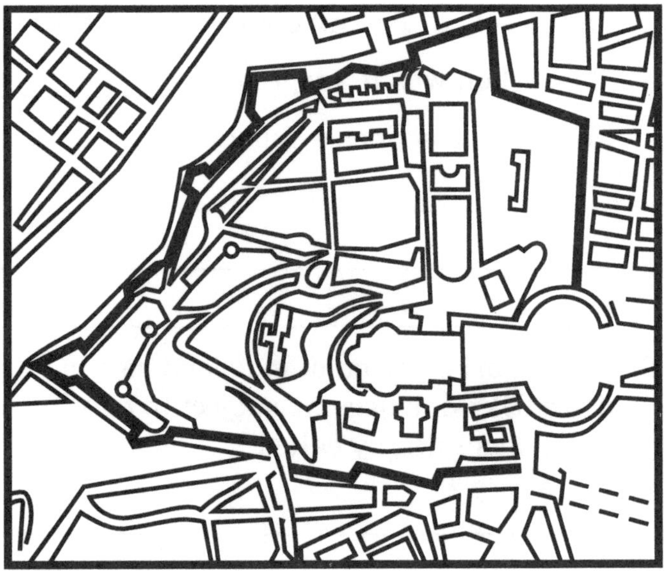

2. Label at least three items on the map, such as Saint Peter's Basilica.
3. Vatican City is located in the city of

   ______________________________ .

   Why was it located there?

   ____

   ____

4. How many acres of land does Vatican City cover? ______________________
5. What is the country's population? ______________________
6. The ruler of Vatican City is ______________________ .
7. What is the official name of Vatican City in Latin? ______________________
8. After you have read about the following places, write two interesting facts about each one.

   Vatican Museum(s): ______________________

   ____

   ____

   Vatican Archive: ______________________

   ____

   ____

   Vatican Library: ______________________

   ____

   ____

Extension: Imagine that you are a resident of Vatican City. What might your occupation be? Write a short story or a diary entry about a day in your life.

Name ____________________

Physical Features and General Information

1. On the map, draw a star to show the location of Yugoslavia's capital. Write its name by the star. Label the countries and sea that border Yugoslavia.
2. List the three major land regions.

____

____

____

3. Describe the climate in each region.

____

____

____

____

____

____

4. Which of Europe's major rivers flows into Yugoslavia? ____________________
5. Define *Iron Gate*. ____________________

____

6. What is the country's official language? ____________________
7. What is its national anthem and what does it mean? ____________________
8. Which two republics make up Yugoslavia? ____________________
9. To whom did the Yugoslavian government provide arms in recent years? Why?

____

____

____

Extension: Pretend that you've been sent by Bosnian Croats to spy on Yugoslavia. Your job is to determine whether its government is secretly supplying Bosnian Serbs with arms. Describe your plan in a top-secret document, detailing how you will enter the country, who you will pose as, and so on.

Teacher's Notes

Answer Key
Europe

Overview of Europe

Name

Physical Features

1. What is Europe's longest river? the Volga River
2. What are the four major land regions of Europe?
   Northwest Mountains — Central Uplands
   Great European Plain — Alpine Mountain System
3. What is a peninsula? A peninsula is land that is surrounded on three sides by water.
4. List the five major European peninsulas.
   Scandinavian — Iberian
   Apennine — Balkin
   Jutland
5. What is Europe's largest lake? the Caspian Sea
   Describe its water. Why is it considered a lake? Although salt water, it is completely surrounded by land.

Extension: Choose a topic such as Europe's climate, landforms, or plant and animal life to research and study. Share your information through a story, report, travel guide, or art activity.

Page 2

Overview of Europe

Name

History and Culture

1. Scientists have found fossils indicating that humans lived in Europe how many years ago? more than one million
2. Where did the first civilizations develop? They developed in the islands of the Aegean Sea, east of Greece
3. What is another name for the Black Death? bubonic plague
   When did it first break out in Europe and how many people did it kill? 1347-1352; 1/4 of Europe's population
4. When did the period known as the Renaissance begin? 1300s
5. When did the great age of European discovery begin? 1400s
6. What is the Helsinki agreement? It is a signed pledge to work for peacekeeping, human rights, and economic cooperation
7. How many languages are spoken in Europe? 50 languages; 100 dialects
8. How many countries are in Europe? 47 (as of 1995)
9. **Use a current atlas or encyclopedia to find recent population figures of Europe. What country has the largest population? How many people live there?**
   Answers will vary, depending on the year.
   What country has the smallest population? How many people live there?
   Answers will vary, depending on the year.
10. What are autobahns? They are high-speed, four-lane highways.
    What is Europe's oldest airline? The Netherlands Royal Dutch Airlines
    What is Telstar I? It was the first space satellite sending live television programs between Europe and the United States.

Extension: Make a time line of events from the European Renaissance.

Page 3

Albania

Name

Physical Features

1. On the map, draw a star to mark the location of the capital of Albania. Write the city's name next to the star.
2. Label the sea and three countries that border Albania.
3. List the country's major rivers that empty into the sea. Draw a star by the only one used for shipping.
   * Buenë
   Drin
   Shkumbin
   Vijosë
4. Draw in the North Albanian Alps on the map using ^^^.
5. Draw a triangle to show where the highest elevation is located. What is the name of this mountain? Mt. Korabit
   What is its elevation in feet? 9,026
   in meters? 2,751
6. List four minerals that are mined in Albania.
   chromite — lignite
   copper — nickel
7. For many years Albania's borders were closed. People were allowed neither in nor out of the country. How do you think this policy was enforced?
   Answers will vary.

   When was this policy changed? 1990-91

Extension: Research the climate of Albania. Explain in a short report how the mountains affect its weather.

Page 4

Albania

Name ____________

History and Culture

1. In the box, draw and correctly color the flag of Albania.
2. What is the name of the ancient tribe that ruled Albania in 300 B.C.? Illyrians
3. List six of the major civilizations that influenced Albania during the years from 300 B.C. to A.D. 1300. Illyrians, Greeks, Romans, Byzantines, Goths, Slavs, Bulgarians, Normans, Serbs
4. Who is Albania's national hero? Scanderberg
5. In recent times, Albania has been occupied by many countries. What country invaded Albania in 1939? Italy
6. Who is Enver Hoxha? He led the resistance movement called the National Liberation Front during WWII. He led the country for the next 40 yrs.
7. Why do you think so many Albanians disliked Communist rule? Answers will vary.

Extension: Albania has many different cultural influences. List three of the ways this could benefit a country. Share with your classmates.

Page 5

Andorra

Name ____________

Physical Features

1. Mark the location of the capital of Andorra on the map with a star. Write the city's name next to the star.
2. Label the countries that border Andorra.
3. What is the area of Andorra in square miles? 175
4. Name a European country that is smaller in area than Andorra. Answers will vary.

   How many square miles smaller is it than Andorra? Answers will vary.
5. Why have Andorra's boundaries changed little? Steep, rocky mountains surround the country.

6. Label the Pyrenees Mountains using ^^^ on the map. Draw a triangle at the location of Andorra's highest peak. Write the name of the peak near the triangle.
7. Andorra's climate is dry and sunny. The average winter temperatures range from 20° F to 30°F. The summer temperatures range from 70° F to 80° F.
8. What is Andorra's leading agricultural product? tobacco

Extension: Tobacco threatens the health of those who use it. What could a person do to discourage farmers from growing tobacco? Make a list of at least three ways to do this, and share your ideas with your classmates.

Page 6

Andorra

Name ____________

History and Culture

1. Andorra has a national and a state flag. In the boxes provided on this page, draw and correctly color each flag.
2. What is the official language of Andorra? Catalan
3. Until 1993, Andorra was ruled by which two heads of state? What country did each represent? Bishop of Urgel - Spain; President of France

   What was the name given these rulers? "princes of Andorra"

   When did the two countries begin jointly ruling Andorra? 1278/1288, when treaties were signed
4. Under Andorra's new constitution, who now heads Andorra's government? Executive Council member
5. When did women win the right to vote in Andorra? 1970

   How many years is this after women in the United States gained the right to vote? 50 years
6. Name Andorra's chief means of income. tourism

national flag

state flag

Extension: What problems do you think might occur when two countries jointly rule another country? Incorporate your ideas into a short story or skit. Or design a poster that details the differences between the two ruling countries.

Page 7

Austria

Name ____________

Physical Features

1. On the map, draw a star to indicate the location of Austria's capital. Write the city's name next to the star.
2. Draw and label Austria's longest river.
3. Austria is a landlocked country. What is the definition of landlocked? completely surrounded by land

   How many countries border Austria? 8 Label them on the map.

4. List and briefly describe Austria's six main land regions.
   the Granite Plateau
   the Eastern Forelands
   the Alpine Forelands
   the Northern Limestone Alps
   the Central Alps
   the Southern Limestone Alps
   Descriptions will vary.
5. Despite Austria's mountainous terrain, it manages to grow enough crops to supply three-quarters of the food needed by its people. Which of Austria's regions is most used for farming? the Eastern Forelands
6. What are the major influences on Austria's climate? warm, moist winds from the Atlantic bring precipitation and moderate temps.; dry winds from the Asian plains blow hot in summer and cold in winter

Extension: Research and then write a report on a well-known river, mountain range, or other physical feature in Austria.

Page 8

Name ______________________

Physical Features and General Information

1. On the map, draw a star to mark the location of Spain's capital city. Write the city's name by the star.
2. Label the three countries and the sea and ocean that border Spain.
3. On the map, draw the boundaries of the seven major land regions and label each one.
4. What is Spain's area in square miles and square kilometers?

   ______________________ sq. miles

   ______________________ sq. kilometers

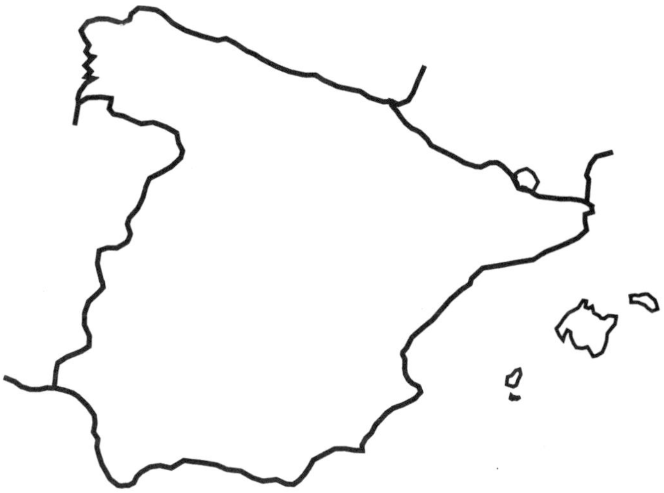

5. On the map, draw and label Spain's two longest rivers.
6. Mark the second largest city with a dot and then write its name.
7. What is Spain's most important natural resource? ______________________
8. Research the Canary Islands. How did they get their name? ______________________

   ____

9. List three facts about the Balearic Islands. Give your source.

   ____

   ____

   ____

   ____

   Source(s): ____ Page(s): __________

10. What natural boundary separates Spain and France? ______________________

Extension: Plan a trip to Spain. Since it is such a large country, you have time to visit only four places. Trace your route on a copy of a map of Spain. Below the map, list and describe your stops. On the map, write the number of miles between consecutive points on your journey. Tell why these places were chosen.

Name ______________________

History

1. In the box, draw and color Spain's flag with its correct colors.

2. What is the national anthem?

   ____

3. What famous non-Spanish explorer started a great age of exploration and conquest for Spain?

   ____

   When did he do this? ______________

4. Name two other explorers of this time and list one accomplishment for each.

   ____

   ____

   ____

5. What was the Spanish Inquisition? ______________________

   ____

6. What caused Spain to lose the empire it had acquired in the 1500s?

   ____

   ____

7. What was the Spanish Armada? What happened to it in 1588?

   ____

   ____

8. What kind of ruler was Francisco Franco? How long did he rule?

   ____

   ____

9. When did Spain begin to establish a democracy? ______________________

   ____

Extension: Read about Spain's role in the American Revolutionary War. Write a letter, detailing Spain's war strategy, from an imaginary Spanish general to George Washington.

Name ______________________

Language

Use a Spanish-English dictionary or encyclopedia to complete the activities below.

1. Write the Spanish words for the numerals one through ten.

______________ ______________ ______________ ______________

______________ ______________ ______________ ______________

______________ ______________

2. Give the meanings of the following Spanish words:

siesta	bueno	madre	gato
______________	______________	______________	______________
mucho	gazpacho	escuela	casa
______________	______________	______________	______________

3. Find two or three advertisements or an article written in Spanish. On another sheet, note and report the words that are similar in both languages. Then have these translated by a Spanish-speaking person.

Food

1. List several foods or drinks we consume that originated in Spain. Use a Spanish cookbook or dictionary if necessary.

______________ ______________ ______________ ______________

______________ ______________ ______________ ______________

2. Why is seafood a staple food in Spain? ______________________________

____

3. Find a recipe for *paella*. Write it on a card to share with others.
4. At what time do urban-dwelling Spanish eat the evening meal? ______________

   What activities do they often do before and after the meal? ______________

   ____

Extension: As a class or family project, plan a meal including only Spanish cuisine. Credit your source for recipes and food ideas.

Name ____________________

Culture

1. Why can ancient Roman ruins be found in parts of Spain? ____________________

2. Describe a typical Spanish workday for city workers. ____________________

3. What is a *paseo*? How does it fit in with the Spanish lifestyle? ____________________

4. How does life in the country differ from that of the city? ____________________

5. Name two important sporting events in Spain. ____________________

6. Spain is rich in artistic traditions. Name several famous artists from Spain.

   Choose one artist on which to research and report.

7. Miguel de Cervantes, a Spanish author, wrote what literary masterpiece? ____________________

   What is the main theme of this literary work? ____________________

8. Read about the music of Spain. Name three world-famous Spanish dances.

   Find tapes or recordings of the type of music that accompanies these dances and share them with classmates.

Extension: Read about Madrid and Barcelona. As an art project, create tourist brochures for these two cities. Include places of interest, historical information, places to dine, and various kinds of recreation and entertainment. Try to include some Spanish words in your brochure. Include illustrations.

Name ______________________

Physical Features

1. On the map, draw a star to mark the location of Sweden's capital city. Write the city's name by the star.
2. Mark with a ● and label three other large cities.
3. Label the countries and the sea and gulf that border Sweden.
4. Name and briefly describe Sweden's four main land regions.

____

____

____

____

____

____

____

____

5. Draw and label on the map the two largest lakes in Sweden.
6. What are Sweden's most important natural resources? ______________________________

____

7. How does Sweden compare in area to the other European countries?

____

8. How does its population compare? ______________________________
9. Research both Sweden's climate and its recreational activities. Tell what time of year you would choose to visit, where you would go, and what activities you would do once there.

____

____

____

10. Sweden is considered a Scandinavian country along with which of its neighbors?

____

Name ______________________

History

1. In the box, draw and correctly color Sweden's flag. When was it first used?

____

2. What is the national anthem?

____

3. Where did the Swedish Vikings explore?

____

4. In early history, what countries made up the Union of Kalmar?

____

5. Who was Gustavus Vasa? What did he do? ______________________

6. Research types of Swedish occupations from the early 1800s to the present. Then write short descriptions of workers from three different time periods. For each worker, include the time period, a made-up Swedish name, his/her occupation, and what work conditions were like.

____

7. What chemical explosive was invented by Alfred Nobel? ______________________

When was it patented? ______________________

Extension: Research important dates in Sweden's history. On a separate sheet of paper, give the dates and historical events that also involved Norway and Denmark.

Name

General Information

1. What is Austria's official language? German

   List three other countries that share this language.

   Germany, Switzerland, Luxembourg, Liechtenstein

2. Austria is a neutral country. Define the word *neutral* and tell how Austria's neutrality is shown.

   neutral- not taking sides; Austria acts as a middleman between Eastern and Western Europe. It is not involved in military affairs.

3. What is the English meaning of the following words?

   chalet: dwelling with a sloping, overhanging roof

   dirndl: full-skirted dress with tight bodice

   Wiener schnitzel: a breaded veal cutlet

4. Austrians enjoy many sports. List at least four. mountain climbing, skiing, ice skating, swimming, hiking, soccer

5. Explain the three options available to students who want to complete their education at a university. complete four years of primary school and nine years high school; complete eight years of primary, one year of prep. & four yrs. high school; eight yrs. primary, five years vocational school

6. Describe Austrian work conditions. Include information on vacations and the length of the workday and workweek.

   Answers may include: 18-day vacations after 6 months of employment; national health care; work weeks never over 40 hours

Extension: Choose an Austrian sport to research and study. Then share your knowledge through a short story or report.

Page 9

Name

History and Culture

1. In the box, draw and correctly color Austria's flag.

2. What is the title of Austria's national anthem?

   "Land der Berge, Land am Strome"

3. When did the Thirty Years' War begin?

   1618

   Briefly tell what the war was about.

   It was fought by Protestant princes against the unity and power of the Holy Roman Empire.

4. What was the Salic law?

   It prohibited women from inheriting a kingdom.

5. Who was Austria's first woman ruler? Maria Theresa

6. What did Austria do in 1955 to obtain independence? Austria agreed to be permanently neutral.

7. Who was Mozart? He was a great musical composer.

   List some of his works. Answers will vary.

8. What Austrian was famous for his waltzes? Johann Strauss

9. What is the meaning of the word *baroque*? It often means an elaborate, highly decorated style.

10. Who is one of Austria's best-known baroque architects?

    Johann Bernhard Fischer von Erlach

Extension: Choose an Austrian artist or musician to research. Find a recording or picture of their work and share it with your class.

Page 10

Name

Physical Features and General Information

1. On the map, draw a star to show the location of the capital. Write the city's name by the star.

2. Label the countries that border Belarus.

3. Most of the land in Belarus is

   lowlands.

4. Belarus has over 10,000 small lakes.

5. List the country's four major rivers.

   1) the Bug
   2) the Dnepr
   3) the Neman
   4) the Western Dvina

6. Belarus declared its independence from Soviet rule in 1991.

7. What is the country's official language? Belarusian

8. What happened in Ukraine in 1986? How did this event affect Belarus?

   Chernobyl nuclear plant exploded causing 70% of the radioactive fallout to be blown by winds to Belarus.

9. What is the education level of most Belarusians? It is very high with most finishing both highschool and college.

10. List the crafts for which Belarus is known. elaborate textiles, straw-inlaid boxes, etc.

11. Briefly describe the lifestyle of the Belarus people.

    Answers will vary.

Page 11

Name

Physical Features

1. On the map, draw a star to indicate the location of the capital of Belgium. Write the city's name next to the star.

2. Label the three countries and the body of water that border Belgium.

3. Using the population guide in an encyclopedia, find Belgium's three largest cities other than the capital. Show their locations on the map using dots. Write each city's name by its dot.

4. Draw the boundaries and label the four main land regions using a red pen, crayon, or marker. Write a brief description of each.

   1) the Coastal and Interior Lowlands
   2) the Kempenland
   3) the Central Low Plateaus
   4) the Ardennes

   Descriptions will vary.

5. What is a *polder*? It is a lowland, extending from the coast. Polders are usually reclaimed land from the sea.

   Where are polders found in Europe besides Belgium?

   Netherlands

6. Describe Belgium's climate and tell how it benefits the country.

   Cool summers and mild winters make for a long, easy growing season. The temperate climate benefits industry as well. (It rarely freezes.)

Page 12

Belgium

Name ____________

History and Culture

1. In the box, draw and correctly color Belgium's flag.

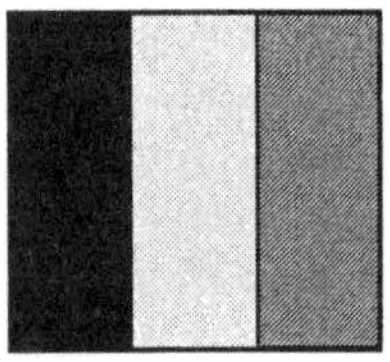

2. What is Belgium's national anthem?
   "La Brabanconne"
3. Who gave Belgium its name?
   Celtic tribes from 100's B.C.
4. Where did Napoleon's final defeat occur?
   The Battle of Waterloo in Central Belgium
5. In 1865, Belgium established the Congo Free State in central Africa. By what name was it known in 1908? the Belgian Congo
   What is it known as today? Zaire
6. What are the two major groups of people in Belgium?
   Flemings   Walloons
   List three ways in which these two groups differ from one another.
   Group 1: Flemings speak Dutch and live mostly in the north. Descended from Germanic Franks.
   Group 2: Walloons speak French and populate the south. Descended from Celts.
7. Briefly describe the Belgians' diet.
   meat dishes, carbonades, waterzooi, French fries, eels, mussels, etc.
8. Belgium has two school systems. What are they called?
   official schools   free schools
9. Name the two famous Belgium surrealist painters from the early 20th century.
   Paul Devaux   René Magritte

Extension: Belgium has many famous artists. Choose one on which to do additional research. Share what you learned through a story, report, play, poster, or other project.

Page 13

Bosnia-Herzegovina

Name ____________

Physical Features and General Information

1. On the map, draw a star to show the location of Bosnia's capital. Write the city's name by the star.
2. Describe the country's two land regions.
   Bosnia - forested and mountainous; Herzegovina - rocky hills, flat farmland
   How do the two differ?
   Bosnia - more trees, higher altitudes; Herzegovina - flatter, agricultural
3. Draw and label the country's four major rivers. Label the countries that border Bosnia-Herzegovina.
4. Draw a ^ to show the country's highest point. Print its name next to the symbol. What is its elevation? 7,828 feet 2,386 meters
5. Bosnia's mountainous land and cold, snowy winters make it a perfect place for skiing.
   Sarajevo hosted the Winter Olympics of what year? 1984
6. From 1918 to 1992, Bosnia was part of a kingdom of Serbs, Croats, and Slovenes who formed what came to be called Yugoslavia through most of the century.
   Bosnia declared its independence from this nation in 1992 against the wishes of the Serbs who declared war on all non-Serbs.
7. Define *ethnic cleansing* as it refers to the struggle in Bosnia. The Serbs believe all non-Serbs must be "purged" from their territories, which often means killing non-Serbs.
8. Most people in Bosnia speak Serbo-Croatian. However, Serbs use the Cyrillic alphabet while Muslims, Croats, and others use the Roman alphabet.

Extension: Research the conflict in Bosnia-Herzegovina by paging through recent news magazines. Make a list of seven things those involved in the conflict could do to prevent such a bloody struggle from ever occurring again.

Page 14

Bulgaria

Name ____________

Physical Features

1. On the map, draw a star to show the location of Bulgaria's capital. Write the city's name next to the star.
2. Label the countries that border Bulgaria.
3. What sea borders Bulgaria to the east?
   the Black Sea
   Label it on the map.
4. What is the largest mountain range that covers Bulgaria?
   The Balkan Mountains
5. Mark the highest peak with the symbol ^ and write its name beside the symbol.
6. What are Bulgaria's two leading grain crops? wheat, corn
7. Name and briefly describe Bulgaria's four land regions.
   1) the Danubian Plateau   Descriptions will vary.
   2) the Balkan Mountains
   3) the Transitional Mountains and Lowlands
   4) the Rhodope Mountains
8. Why does Bulgaria's climate vary so much from region to region?
   The terrains vary.
9. Where is Bulgaria's most popular vacation area? Why?
   The Black Sea coast boasts beautiful beaches and mild weather.

Extension: Pretend you are climbing Bulgaria's highest peak. Write a story about your climb. Include such details as what you will bring and how long your climb will take.

Page 15

Bulgaria

Name ____________

History and Culture

1. In the box, draw and color the flag. How has it changed in the last few years?
   The star representing communism has been taken off.

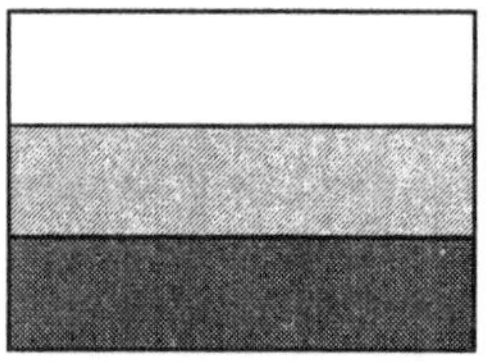

2. Why were the Thracians important to Bulgaria's history?
   They established the first civilization in Bulgaria.
3. How long did Turkish rule last in Bulgaria? over 500 years
4. Why did Bulgaria enter World War I and World War II?
   Bulgaria wanted to regain territory lost during the second Balkan war and then further territory lost during WWI.
5. By what year was Bulgaria totally controlled by the Communists? 1948
6. List some of the minority groups that make up Bulgaria.
   Turks, Armenians, Greeks, Gypsies, Macedonians, Russians, Romanians
7. What is Bulgaria's official language? Bulgarian
   To what other language is it similar? Russian
8. Bulgaria has a literacy rate of 98 percent. Define *literacy*.
   It is the ability to read and write.

Extension: Read about the Bulgaria of today in newspapers and current news magazines. Incorporate this information into a poster that compares the old Bulgaria with the new.

Page 16

Croatia

Name

Physical Features and General Information

1. On the map, draw a star to show the location of Croatia's capital. Write the city's name by the star.
2. List and describe Croatia's two land regions. Dalmatia - coastal region of rocky cliffs and little fertile soil. Pannonian Plains - area of fertile soil in the north
3. The Dinaric Alps run through the country's center. Mark them on the map using the symbol ʍʌ.
4. What is a *bora*? Cold, gusty wind that sometimes blows down from the mountains in northern areas
5. Why did war break out in 1991? Serbs resisted Croatia's independence from the former Yugoslavia. Serbs wished to unify all Serbs and expand their territory.
6. What are the two major ethnic groups in Croatia? Croats and Serbs
7. Croatian is the official language and is actually so much like Serbian that some linguists consider them dialects of a single language called Serbo-Croatian. How do these two language forms differ and why do you think Croats wish to distinguish them further? Croatian is written in the Roman alphabet and Serbian in the Cyrillic. Croats want to define their ethnic identity.
8. How did the recent war affect where Croats live? Croats living in the country and small villages fled to cities.
9. How has rock music played a role in recent Croatian history? Rock musicians sang songs of protest during Communist rule.

Page 17

Czech Republic

Name

Physical Features

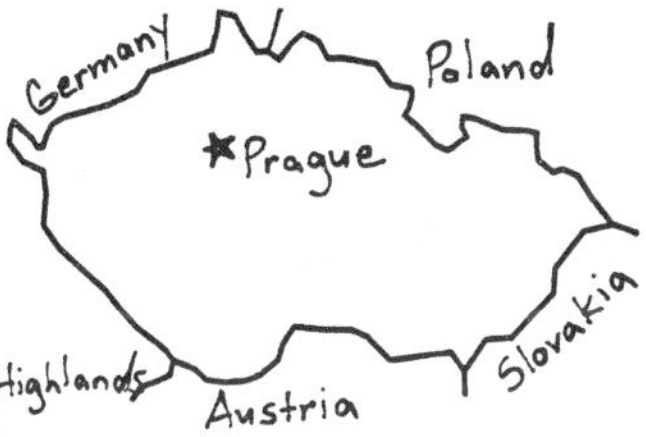

1. On the map, draw a star to show the location of the capital of the Czech Republic. Write the city's name by the star.
2. Label the four countries that border the Czech Republic.
3. Name the country's five land regions.
   1) the Bohemian Mts.
   2) the Sudeten Mts.
   3) the Bohemian Basin
   4) the Bohemian-Moravian Highlands
   5) the Moravian Lowlands

   Choose one of the regions and write a short description. Answers will vary.
4. **Name two leading manufacturing cities in the Czech Republic.** Others possible. Brno, Hradec Králové, Ostrava, Plzeň
5. What are some of the major crops grown in this country? List at least four. barley, corn, fruit, hops, oats, potatoes, wheat, vegetables
6. What plagues one of the country's largest nature preserves in the Krkonose Mountains? Where do you think this problem most likely originated? Acid rain and other pollution hurts plants and animals. The pollutants originate from industry in the south.

Extension: Research the Czech Republic's land regions. Then write a travelogue about your trip to one or more of these land regions. Incorporate facts into your travelogue.

Page 18

Czech Republic

Name

History

1. In the box, draw and correctly color the Czech Republic's flag.

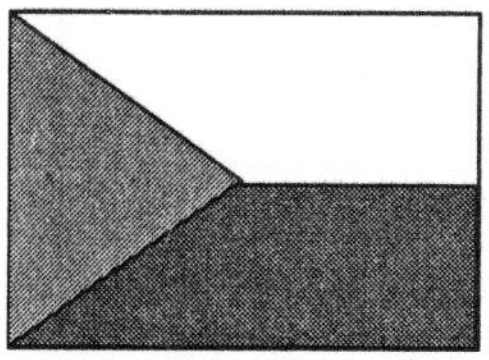

2. When was this area first settled? A.D. 500

   Who were the first settlers? Slavic tribes
3. What is the Czech Republic's national anthem? "Kde domov muj?" ("Where is my home?")
4. Who was Alexander Dubcek? He was a Slovak who became a Communist party leader. He introduced "Prague spring," or "socialism with a human face" and other liberal reforms
5. The Czech Republic was once part of what country? Czechoslovakia

   When did it become independent? 1992
6. Václav Havel was a non-communist playwright who served as president of the former Czechoslovakia in the early 1990s. Would such a person ever hold this position in your country? Explain. Answers will vary.
7. What was the Velvet Revolution and how did it get its name? It was the end of Communist rule; it was "velvet" because it was so peaceful.
8. What is the traditional Czech meal at Christmas? carp with potato salad
9. *New Wave* refers to which Czech art of the 1960s? film making

   Describe the goal of this art form. The art form critiqued social and political conditions.

Extension: A modern renaissance is occurring in the city of Prague. Research this renaissance in news magazines or other sources and write a skit illustrating it.

Page 19

Denmark

Name

Physical Features

1. On the map, draw a star to show the location of the capital of Denmark. Write the city's name next to the star.
2. Mark the location of Denmark's three largest cities, other than the capital, by drawing a dot with the city's name written next to each.
3. Label the country that borders Denmark.
4. Denmark consists of a large peninsula and many islands. Name the peninsula. Jutland

   Approximately how many islands make up Denmark? 482
5. Denmark's land is covered by a material called *moraine*. Define moraine. Moraine is earth and stone left by glaciers melting thousands of years ago.
6. Name Denmark's land regions. 1) the Western Dune Coast 2) the Western Sand Plains 3) the East-Central Hills 4) the Northern Flat Plains 5) Bornholm

   Describe one of these regions. Answers will vary.
7. What is the chief cause of Denmark's mild, damp climate? It is surrounded by water.

Extension: Research transportation in Denmark. Then pretend that you are leading a group of bicyclists from Copenhagen to Alborg with a stop in Odense. Trace your route in pencil on the map above. On a separate sheet, tell about your tour. Include answers to the following questions. How many kilometers will you travel? How will you get your bicycles across the Great Belt (channel)?

Page 20

Name

History and Culture

1. In the box, draw and correctly color the flag of Denmark.

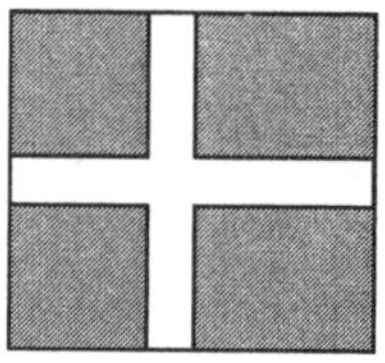

2. Who was King Harald Bluetooth? He united Denmark in A.D. 950 and introduced Christianity.
3. What was the Union of Kalmar? Queen Margaret united Denmark, Norway, and Sweden in 1397.
4. Describe Denmark's role in World War II. In 1940 German forces invaded Denmark and Danes soon surrendered. However, a strong and effective resistance movement enabled 7,000 Danish Jews to escape.
5. What famous person from Denmark wrote fairy tales? Hans Christian Anderson
   List four stories written by this author. Answers will vary.
6. What kind of food is *smørrebrød*? They are pretty, open-faced sandwiches served at meals.
7. After reading about Denmark, explain why each of the following items could be included in a poster on Denmark.
   a. stork symbol of good luck; storks build nests on roof tops.
   b. Viking Danish Vikings trampled Europe and conquered Engl.
   c. soccer ball Soccer is Denmark's most popular sport.
   d. Tivoli Gardens It is a famous Copenhagen amusement park
   e. Storstrøm Bridge It is one of the longest bridges in Europe.
   f. barley Denmark is one of world's major barley producers.

   Design a travel poster and include information on at least three of the items.

Name

Physical Features and General Information

1. On the map, draw a star to indicate the location of the capital of Estonia. Write the city's name next to the star.
2. Label the countries that border Estonia.
3. Label the Baltic Sea, the Gulf of Finland, and the Gulf of Riga.
4. Estonia's land is chiefly a low plain.
5. Read about the climate of Estonia and explain it in your own words. It has an unusually mild climate for a northern area; its air is affected by ocean breezes. In January temperatures average 19°-28°F. In July temperatures range from 61°-64°
   Why is this climate unusual for its location? See above answer. It's unually mild for northern area.
6. Do most Estonians live in urban or rural areas? urban
7. Most Estonians work in manufacturing or mining.
8. In the box, draw and color Estonia's flag. Explain the meaning of each of the colors.
   blue = sky
   black = land
   white = the future.

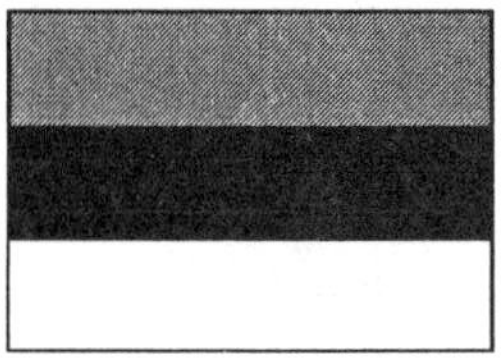

Name

Physical Features

1. On the map, draw a star to indicate the location of Finland's capital. Write the city's name next to the star.
2. Label the Gulf of Bothnia and the Gulf of Finland.
3. Label the countries that border Finland.
4. Using a dashed line (--------), show where the Arctic Circle crosses Finland. Why is the area inside the Arctic Circle known as the "Land of the Midnight Sun"? In the Arctic Circle the sun shines for 24 hours a day during much of the summer.
5. What is the *aurora borealis*? northern lights—caused by electrically charged particles from the sun, which create dramatic and colorful displays of light.
   What is another name for the aurora borealis? northern lights
6. What covers more than two-thirds of the land in Finland? forests
7. What type of power provides half of Finland's electricity? water power
8. List at least two Finnish industries and tell how they relate to Finland's natural resources. plywood manufactured with wood from Finland's forests shipbuilding - ferries and icebreakers travel Finland's frozen waters to neighboring areas.

Extension: Choose a specific physical feature of Finland to research. Share your information through an illustrated poster.

Name

History and Culture

1. In the box, draw and correctly color Finland's flag.

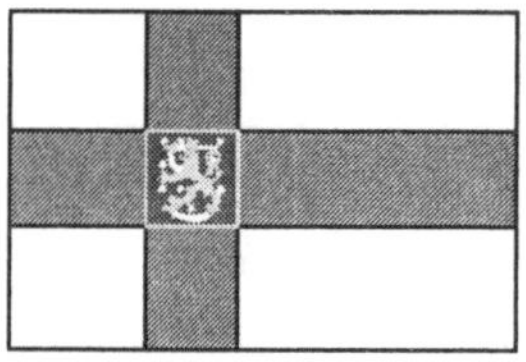

2. Who were the first people known to have lived in Finland? Lapps
   When did the ancestors of present-day Finns begin to arrive? thousands of years ago
3. What countries once fought over possession of Finland? Sweden and Russia
4. What are the two official languages of Finland? Write the percentage of people who speak each one.
   a. Finnish 95 %
   b. Swedish 5 %
5. What is Finland's name in Finnish? Suomi
6. What is a *sauna*? What has it to do with Finland? A sauna is a very popular hot bathing room in which stones are heated.
7. Who was Elias Lönnrot? Why is he important to Finnish culture? He was a country doctor who preserved the old poems, chants, and oral history of Finnish peasants. In 1835, he published Kalevala, Finlands national epic.
8. List three of the social welfare programs of Finland. health coverage, pensions for old and disabled, new baby allowances, free health care for children, 26-day vacations if employed for one year, etc.
9. Finland is the world's leading producer of what building material? plywood
10. Who is Finalnd's present head of state? Answers will vary.

Finland

Finnish Foods

Name ______

1. In Finland, kropsu is served at morning and afternoon work breaks, especially to those people working in the fields. Try the recipe below.

Finnish Kropsu

- 3 large eggs
- ½ cup sugar
- ¾ cup flour
- ¼ teaspoon salt
- ¼ pound butter or margarine (one stick)

Beat eggs and sugar until well-blended. Add flour and salt and mix well. Melt the butter in a small sauce pan. Add the melted butter to the batter and beat well. Blend in the milk. Pour the batter into a 9- x 13-inch pan and bake in a 400° oven until browned and set, about 30-40 minutes.

The dough will puff up while cooling but fall when cooling. Cut in squares and eat by hand or serve on a plate. If desired, top with whipped cream and sliced fruit.

2. What are some other Finnish foods? herring, perch, pike, salmon, boiled potatoes with butter and dill
3. What meat is considered a special treat in Finland? smoked reindeer

Extension: Make up your own Finnish trivia game. Play the game at a Finnish theme party at which Kropsu is served.

Page 25

France

Physical Features

Name ______

1. On the map, draw a star to indicate the location of the capital of France. Write the city's name by the star.
2. Label the countries that border France.
3. Draw and label the three main rivers that run through France.
4. On the map, draw and label the highest mountains in France.
5. How many main land regions are there in France? 10

   Name and then describe the region in which you would most enjoy living if you were to move to France. Explain why.

   Answers will vary.
6. What is the Riviera? What affects its climate?

   It is a coastal area in southwest France affected by warm breezes of Mediterranean Sea and sheltered from north winds by the Alps.
7. Name France's most important natural resource. What is its primary use?

   fertile soil used for agriculture
8. Write the name and give a brief description of one of France's famous caves.

   Answers will vary.

Extension: Pretend that you and a friend have just discovered a new cave. Write a short story about your adventure.

Page 26

France

History and Culture

Name ______

1. What is the name of France's flag?

   the tricolor

   Draw and correctly color the flag in the box.

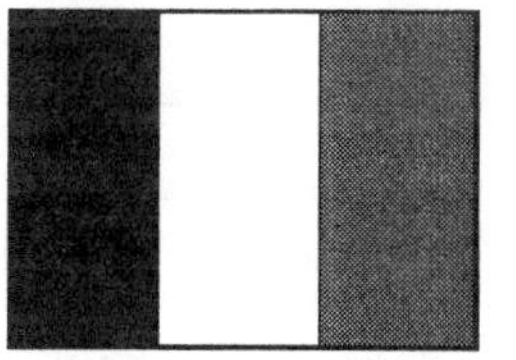

2. What is the national anthem?

   "La Marseillaise"
3. In ancient times, tribes of Celts and other peoples lived in the region now called France. What did the Romans call this region? Gallia (Gaul)
4. Napoleon Bonaparte was considered an excellent administrator. List at least two reasons why.

   He created a strong central government organized French law, organized French military, etc.
5. What is the Tour de France? It is a cross-country bicycle race.
6. Explain how the United States became the home of the French-produced Statue of Liberty.

   France presented it to the U.S. in 1884 as a gift of friendship and a symbol of liberty.
7. Name at least one French painter known for each of the following art styles.

   Impressionism Manet, Pissarro, Degas, Monet, Renoir, etc.

   Neoclassicism David

   Romanticism Gericault, Delacroix, Rousseau, etc.

   Postimpressionism Cézanne, Gauguin, Seurat, Toulouse-Lautrec

   Surrealism Masson

   Cubism Braque

Extension: Draw a picture on another sheet of paper that relates to the culture of France. Use the style of a famous French artist. Name the artist and the style you chose.

Page 27

France

Language

Name ______

Use a French dictionary, an encyclopedia, or other source to complete the activities below.

1. Write the correct numeral above each French number word. Identify your source.

10 dix	1 un	9 neuf
2 deux	8 huit	5 cinq
4 quatre	6 six	3 trois
7 sept	Source: ______	

2. Write the French number words in the correct order. Add a comma between each number.

   un, deux, trois, quatre, cinq, six, sept, huit, neuf, dix
3. Draw at least three objects in the box below and label them in English and in French. You may use the back of this paper if you want to draw and label more objects. Make sure the words are spelled correctly. Learn the correct pronunciations.

   Source: ______ Page(s): ______

   Answers will vary.

Page 28

France

Name ______________

Eiffel Tower

1. In which city is the Eiffel Tower located? *Paris*

   When was it built? *1889*

   What is its height? *984 feet*

2. List the Eiffel Tower's features and tell why it was built. *Answers will vary.*

3. Why do you think the Eiffel Tower is so famous? *Answers will vary.*

4. Imagine that you are standing by the Eiffel Tower. Describe what you might see and do there. *Answers will vary.*

Page 29

Germany

Name ______________

Physical Features

1. On the map, draw a star to show the location of Germany's capital. Write the city's name next to the star. Use dots to show the location of four other German cities. Label each. *Cities will vary.*
2. Label the countries and seas that border Germany.
3. How long is the Rhine River in standard and in metric measurements? *820 miles/1,320 Kilo.*

   Draw and label this river.
4. Briefly describe the Bavarian Alps. *The mountains were cut by ancient glaciers which left lakes when the ice melted.*

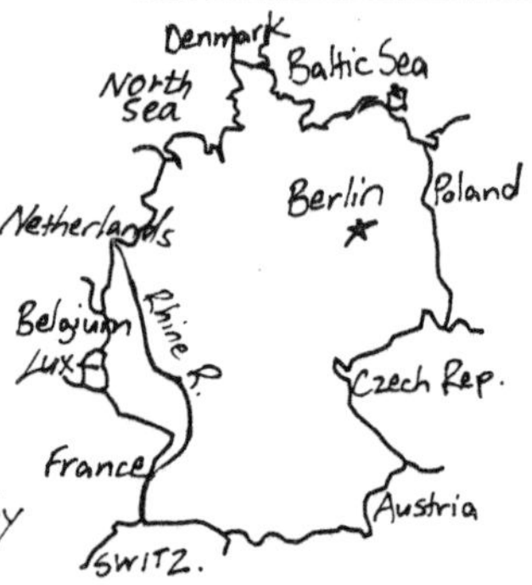

5. Name Germany's highest peak and give its height. *Zugspitze - 9,721 ft. / 2,963 m.*
6. Name and describe Germany's largest land region. *The North German Plain covers northern Germany. It lies 300 ft. above sea level and is drained by several rivers.*
7. Read about the trees in the Black Forest. List two kinds of trees that grow there. *dark fir and spruce*

Extension: Draw and color a leaf and/or branch from each Black Forest tree you listed above. Label each.

Page 30

Germany

Name ______________

History

1. In the box, draw and correctly color the German flag.

2. What was the Reformation? *It was the beginning of Protestantism begun by Martin Luther, who protested abuses in the church.*
3. Briefly describe Germany's role in World War I. *It joined with Austria-Hungary when it declared war on Serbia and declared war on Russia when it sided with Serbia. It was one of the Central Powers. Answers may vary.*
4. When Adolf Hitler came into power, he pursued two goals. What were they? List two or three ways in which he set out to accomplish these goals. *They were to assert German superiority over what he called inferior races such as Jews and Slavs and to gain territory for Germany, especially in eastern Europe. Methods will vary.*
5. Briefly explain when and why the wall was built between East and West Berlin. *The wall was built in 1961 to keep East Germans from crossing over into the West where the living conditions were much better.*

Extension: Research the Holocaust and write an essay answering the following: What was the Holocaust? How do you think such a thing could have occurred in this century in a country of well-educated people? Could it happen in your country? Explain.

Page 31

Germany

Name ______________

Culture

1. Germany's most popular organized sport is *soccer*.
2. List at least six other sports or activities Germans enjoy doing during their leisure time. *hiking, reading, gardening, swimming, bicycling, hitchhiking trips, etc.*
3. Write three facts on one of the following German composers: Bach, Beethoven, Brahms, or Wagner. *Answers will vary.*

   Source: ______________ Page(s): ______
4. Read about a German artist. Then list the title of one of his art pieces and the name of the museum where it is located. *Answers will vary.*
5. What was the *Bauhaus*? *It is an international school of modern design started by Walter Gropius, a German who introduced interior open space concept.*
6. Germany is known for introducing several well-known foods. Name four. *Answers will vary.*
7. If you were to visit Germany, what would you like to see or do? *Answers will vary.*

Extension: Research Neuschwanstein Castle. Find out what is unique about it and design a modern version that also has unusual features. Show a cut-away view of the interior with labels for each room and feature.

Page 32

Germany

Name ____________

Language

Refer to a German dictionary, an encyclopedia, or other source to complete the activities below.

1. Write the correct numeral above each German number word. List your source.

5 fünf	8 acht	1 ein
10 zehn	3 drei	9 neun
2 zwei	6 sechs	4 vier
7 sieben	Source: ____________	

2. Write the German number words in the correct order. Add a comma between each number.
ein, zwei, drei, vier, fünf, sechs, sieben, acht, neun, zehn

3. Draw at least three objects in the box below and label them in English and in German. You may use the back of this page if you want to draw and label more objects. Make sure the words are spelled correctly. Learn the correct pronunciations.

Source: ____________ Page(s): ____________

Answers will vary.

Page 33

Great Britain

Name ____________

Physical Features

1. On the map, draw a star to show the location of Great Britain's capital. Write the city's name by the star.
2. Draw and label the two longest rivers in Great Britain.
3. The official name of this nation is "The United Kingdom of Great Britain and Northern Ireland," but most people call this country one of these three names:
Great Britain,
United Kingdom,
Britain

4. What body of water separates Great Britain from France?
the English Channel
How has this body of water helped Great Britain?
It provided security during war and helped England develop its own character.
5. Name Great Britain's land regions.
1) the Scottish Highlands 2) the Central Lowlands 3) the Central Uplands 4) the Pennines 5) Wales 6) the Southwest Peninsula 7) the English Lowlands 8) Northern Ireland
Pick two of the regions that most interest you and explain why.
Answers will vary.

Extension: Research both Great Britain's climate and that of Labrador, Canada. Compare the latitudes of these two places. Why do these two locations have such vastly different climates?

Page 34

Great Britain

Name ____________

History

1. In the box, draw and color Great Britain's flag. In what year was it officially adopted?
1801

2. The national anthem of Great Britain is
"God Save the Queen/King"
3. What is the basic unit of money in Great Britain? pound
4. How is the "throne" passed from one person to another in Great Britain?
The throne passes from the reigning monarch to the eldest son. If there are no male children, the eldest daughter inherits the throne
5. How did the Victorian Age get its name?
It was named after Queen Victoria who reigned from 1837-1901, the longest rule in British history.
During the Victorian Age, the British Empire included what fraction of the world's land and people? 1/4
6. List the six large countries that were British colonies up until 1931 when they gained independence. Republic of Ireland, Australia, Canada, New Zealand, NewFoundland, South Africa
These six countries became the first members of the Commonwealth of Nations.
8. Describe Great Britain's role in World War II. Great Britain was the only European country to stand fast against Nazi military strength. With the U.S. they liberated Europe.
9. Which British leader inspired and unified both his people and other allies in the effort to win World War II? Winston Churchhill

Page 35

Great Britain

Name ____________

Culture

1. The most popular sport in Great Britain is soccer.

What are some other favorite sports and pastimes of the British?
crisket, golf, hockey, horseback riding, sailing, horse racing, rugby, tennis
2. The British Museum in London has many wonderful treasures such as the Rosetta Stone from Egypt and the Elgin Marbles from the Parthenon in Athens. Write a brief description of these two items.
The Rosetta Stone is a black basalt rock covered in hieroglyphics, Demotic, & Greek inscriptions. The Elgin Marbles are marble scultures from the Acropolis in Athens.
3. What is the largest library in Great Britain? the British Library
4. Identify Great Britain's grammar schools, independent schools, and public schools.
grammar schools - specialize in college preparation
independent schools - private schools charging tuition
public schools - independent schools, originally established for the poor
5. Who was William Shakespeare? List two of his works.
England's, and perhaps the world's most famous playwright. Answers on works will vary.
6. For what goods are each of the following countries known?
Wales: coal, livestock, slate, shale
England: clothing, processed foods, agriculture, oil
Scotland: whisky, livestock, coal, fish
Northern Ireland: livestock, potatoes, limestone, dairy

Extension: The British have made major contributions to rock music. Research a British band and write a magazine article outlining the group's history.

Page 36

Great Britain

Name ______________

Big Ben

1. Some tourists who go to Europe want to see Big Ben. What is it? Big Ben is the great bell in the Clock tower of the houses of Parliament.
2. Big Ben is located in what city? London
3. How did Big Ben get its name? The bell was installed when Sir Benjamin Hall was commissioner of works. Sir Hall was a big man nicknamed Big Ben; the bell was named after him.
4. How much does Big Ben weigh? 5 short tons
5. Draw Big Ben on the tower in the illustration.
6. If you were to travel to Europe, would you like to see Big Ben? Why, or why not? Answers will vary.
7. Pretend that you have been given the job of cleaning Big Ben. How would you go about this interesting but challenging task? Answers will vary.

Extension: On another sheet, draw a picture of the place that you would most like to visit in Great Britain.

Page 37

Greece

Name ______________

Physical Features

1. On the map, draw a star to mark the location of the capital of Greece. Write the city's name by the star.
2. Write the names of the following seas on the map where they are located: Aegean, Ionian, Mediterranean, Sea of Crete.
3. What is the Peloponnesus? It is a large peninsula covered with mountains and dramatic coastline. It is very important historically. Label it on the map.
4. Label the countries that border Greece.
5. Of what stone is much of Greece's land composed? limestone
6. What is *maquis*? It is the thorny, woody shrub that covers much of Greece.
7. What is Greece's tallest mountain? Write its height in standard and metric measurements. Mt. Olympus; 9570 ft. (2,917 m) Why is this mountain so famous? It figures prominently in Greek myths, history, and religion.
8. What makes the island of Ithaca a tourist attraction? It was the home of Ulysses in the epic poem the Odyssey.
9. Write an interesting fact about the Greek islands. Answers will vary. Source: ______________ Page(s): ______________
10. Choose a specific island, set of islands, river, mountain, coastline, or other physical feature to study and report on to others.

Page 38

Greece

Name ______________

History and Culture

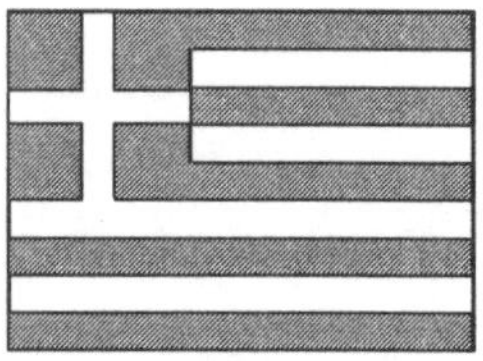

1. In the box, draw and correctly color the flag. What do the stripes represent? blue stripes = sea and sky white stripes = Greek struggle for independence
2. Who was the great leader who conquered the Greeks and became their first king in 338 B.C.? Philip II of Macedonia
3. Who was the son of the above ruler? What was his major accomplishment? Alexander the Great; he conquered the Persian Empire extending the Greek empire from Greece to India.
4. List at least two reasons why the Parthenon is highly regarded. Possible answers: 1) It is an ancient Greek temple honoring Athena. 2) Made of white marble, it had to be carted 11 miles to a building site
5. What contributions have the ancient Greek civilization given to our civilization? contributed to art, architecture, math, science, philosophy, politics, etc.
6. What are the *Iliad* and the *Odyssey*? The Iliad is Homer's tale of the Trojan War. The Odyssey is Homer's tale of Odysseus' ten-year adventure.
7. Many modern Greeks dance to folk music featuring what two instruments? the clarinet and the bouzouki
8. What is the Greek's favorite meat? lamb List the ingredients found in *dolmathes* and *moussaka*. vine leaves filled with rice and ground meat (dolmathes); layers of eggplant and ground meat (moussaka).

Page 39

Greece

Name ______________

Art

After studying Ancient and Modern Greece, draw pictures representing each period.

Ancient Greece

Pictures will vary.

Modern Greece

Page 40

Greece

Name ______________

Olympic Games

1. The Olympic Games originated in ancient Greece. What Greek god was honored at the ceremonies? *Zeus*
2. What did a winning participant of the ancient Olympics receive? *laurel leaf crown*
3. Why did the ancient Olympics end? When did the modern Olympics begin? *The Romans conquered Greece; 1896*
4. Under what name did the athletes from the group of former Soviet states compete under in 1992? *the Unified Team*
5. Imagine you have just won a gold medal. What sport did you win it in? Write a short story or report about your Olympic experience.

Extension: Pick a European country that has competed in the Olympics. Research the events, athletes, or special occurrences of a specific year. Present your findings by reenacting a portion of that year's Olympic Games.

Page 41

Hungary

Name ______________

Physical Features

1. On the map, draw a star to mark the location of the capital of Hungary. Write the city's name by the star.
2. Label the countries that border Hungary.
3. On the map, draw and label the Danube River. Write three facts about this river. *Answers will vary.*

4. Name and describe the largest lake in Hungary. Label it on the map. *Lake Balaton - the largest lake in central Europe; it is a popular recreation and vacation spot.*
5. List the names of the four main land regions of Hungary: *The Great Plain* *Transdanubia* *The Little Plain* *The Northern Highlands*
   Choose one of these regions and write a brief description. *Answers will vary.*
6. What are Hungary's two most important natural resources? Why are they important? *fertile soil - agriculture* *climate - agriculture*

Extension: Choose a specific topic on the physical features of Hungary to research. Then share this information through your own travelogue that includes illustrations.

Page 42

Hungary

Name ______________

History and Culture

1. In the box, draw and color the Hungarian flag with its correct colors.
2. List two important dates in Hungary's history and describe the events that took place on these dates. *Answers will vary.*

3. Write the name of the first king of Hungary. Describe his rule. *Stephen I made Roman Catholicism the country's official religion. Unified Maygar tribes into a nation.*
4. In 1989, Hungary made major changes in its *constitution*. How did this affect the country? *Answers will vary.*
5. Define *spa*. How is this part of Hungary's culture? *It is a health resort offering medicinal bathing in mineral waters. Important activity.*
6. List some other activities people in Hungary enjoy doing for recreation. *soccer, swimming, boating, fishing, basketball, fencing*
7. If you lived in Hungary, what would you do for recreation? *Answers will vary.*
8. Pick one of Hungary's well-known composers. Write at least three facts about this person. *Answers will vary.*

Source: ______________ Page(s): ______________

Page 43

Iceland

Name ______________

Physical Features

1. On the map, draw a star to mark the location of the capital of Iceland. Write the city's name next to the star.
2. Label the bodies of water that surround this island.
3. Label Iceland's largest glacier.

4. Why is Iceland called the "Land of Ice and Fire"? *The land has been shaped by glaciers which still cover 1/8 of Iceland's area. It gets its "fire" from its numerous volcanoes, some still active.*
5. Why is Iceland sometimes referred to as a land of "midnight sun"? *In June it is light 24 hrs./day.*
6. What is the only habitable area in Iceland? Why? *The lowlands are the only habitable area; they are warmer, grass grows there along with sheep and some crops.*
7. What is *Geysir*? *It is Iceland's famous hot spring which spouts water 195 feet into the air.*
8. Describe the features of Iceland's inland plateau. *rugged, barren* *2,500 feet above sea level* *crossed by faultline* *home to volcanoes, hot springs, geysers, glaciers, and lava fields*

Extension: Prepare an oral report on one of the following topics that relates to Iceland: volcano, geyser, glacier, earthquake, or fault line.

Page 44

Iceland

Name ______

History and Culture

1. In the box, draw and correctly color the flag of Iceland.

2. Who began Icelandic settlement in about A.D. 870? *Ingolfur Arnason*
3. What was the "Althing"? *the world's first parliament – in Iceland*
4. When did Iceland officially become independent? *June 17, 1944*
5. Iceland has had numerous disasters. Name one of these disasters. Then explain how you would have tried to cope with this disaster if you had been there at the time. *Answers will vary.*
6. How do children in Iceland's isolated areas receive an education? *They ride buses or attend boarding schools. In some isolated areas, teachers travel from farm to farm.*
7. Why is it so expensive to live in Iceland? *Everything must be imported.*
8. List at least five things that Icelanders like to do during their leisure time. *swimming, basketball, handball, skiing, soccer, glima*
9. How do Icelanders name their children? *They give a first name and then a second name that combines the father's first name and "son," if a boy or "dottir," if a girl.*

Extension: Read as much as possible about Iceland. Then compare and contrast living in Iceland to where you live.

Page 45

Ireland

Name ______

Physical Features

1. On the map, draw a star to mark the location of Ireland's capital. Write the city's name next to it.
2. Draw a dot to show the location of the following cities/towns: Cork, Killarney, Limerick, Tipperary. Label each.
   Which one of these cities/towns would you most like to visit? *Answers will vary.*
   Why? ______
3. Label Northern Ireland.
4. The *Irish* Sea and *St. George's* Channel separate Ireland from Great Britain to the east while the *North Atlantic* Ocean borders Ireland on the north, south, and west. Label these on the map.
5. Why is Ireland called the *Emerald Isle*? *lush, green countryside*
6. What fraction of the island of Ireland is occupied by the country of Ireland? *5/6*
   What fraction is occupied by Northern Ireland? *1/6*
7. Read as much as possible about the natural and man-made physical features of Ireland. Then write 20 words or phrases that relate to this topic. Separate the words and phrases with commas. *Words will vary.*

Extension: Peat bogs cover about a tenth of Ireland. Pretend that you are a famous scientist who wishes to study these bogs in order to come up with a new use for them. Write a one-page proposal outlining your project.

Page 46

Ireland

Name ______

History and Culture

1. In the box, draw and color the Irish flag in its correct colors.

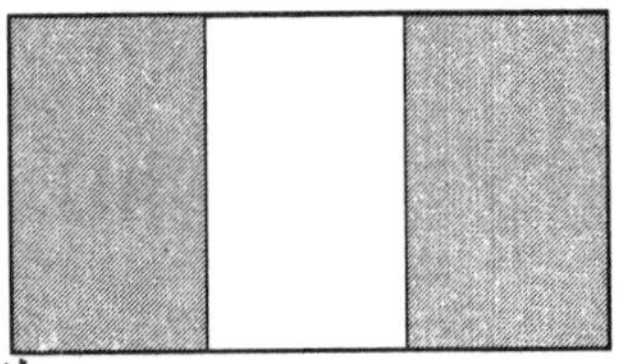

2. Give the origins of Saint Patrick's Day. *St. Patrick, the patron saint of Ireland, came to Ireland as a missionary in A.D. 432. His feast day, March 17, is a national holiday.*
3. Write a brief description of the potato famine that took place during the 1800s. *Many Irish families lived on small farms and grew potatoes as their main food source. Between 1845-1847, the crop failed causing starvation and disease.*
4. Read about the Blarney Stone. Explain its legend. *A woman cast a good spell on a king who saved her from drowning; when he kissed the stone, he spoke eloquently.*
6. What are the two official languages of Ireland? *Gaelic and English*
7. List at least three sports that are popular in Ireland. *horseback riding, horse racing, soccer, cricket, rugby*
8. Who was the famous tenor that made Irish folk music popular? *John McCormack*
   If possible, find and listen to some music by this person.
9. Ireland produced many great writers during a period known as the Irish Literary Revival. Name two of these writers and list one or more of each of their works. *Answers will vary.*
10. Why is the shamrock synonymous with Ireland? *The three-leaved plants cover Ireland and are said to be chosen by St. Patrick as a symbol of the trinity. Shamrocks are the national plant.*

Extension: Research Irish poetry and recite some Irish poems to an audience of your choosing.

Page 47

Ireland

Name ______

Collage on Ireland

Read as much as possible about Ireland in encyclopedias and other reference books. Then make a collage portraying Ireland and its people. Cut and laminate the square or cover with contact paper and use it as a mat for a plant such as a shamrock.

Collages will vary.

Page 48

Italy

Name ________

Physical Features

1. On the map, draw a star to show the location of Italy's capital. Write the city's name by the star.
2. Label the countries and the seas that border Italy.
3. What is the approximate length and width (at the widest point) of Italy?
   length - 708 mi. (1,139 Km)
   width - 320 mi. (515 Km.)
4. List the six land regions of Italy excluding the islands.
   1) the Alpine Slope
   2) the Po Valley
   3) the Adriatic Plain
   4) the Apennines
   5) Apulia and Southeastern Plains
   6) the Western Uplands and Plains

   If you were able to go to only one of these regions, which one would it be and why?
   Answers will vary.
5. Name the two island regions. Sicily and Sardinia
   Label them on the map.
6. Italy is shaped like what kind of footwear? a boot
7. Describe Italy's climate. It is sunny every season but winter.
8. Which mountain range attracts many skiers? the Alps

Extension: Choose one of the following topics to study: Alps, Apennine Tunnel, Arno River, Brenner Pass, Lake Como, Lake Maggiore, Matterhorn, Bay of Naples, Po River, Saint Bernard Passes, Tiber River, Tyrol, or Vesuvius. Take notes and write a report.

Page 49

Italy

Name ________

History and Culture

1. Who designed the Italian flag?
   Napolean Bonaparte
   In the box, draw and color the flag.

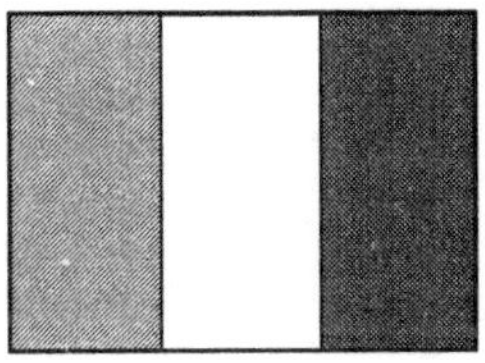

2. Ancient Rome is very important in Italy's history. Explain why.
   Answers will vary.
3. What is the basic unit of money in Italy? lira
4. Compare and contrast a popular way to travel in Venice to a popular way to travel in your area. Venice - water bus, gondola, on foot
   most other areas - bus, car, train, on foot
5. What is an opera? It is a drama in which song and orchestral music is the main vehicle.
   When and where were the first operas composed? In 1590, the first operas were composed in Florence.
   Name four famous Italian composers. Verdi, Puccini, Bellini, Donizetti, Rossini
6. Many famous artists were born and/or studied in Italy. Name at least six Italian artists.
   Answers will vary.

   Choose one of these artists and write a short paragraph about that person, including the names of some of his works.
   Answers will vary.

Page 50

Italy

Name ________

Pictorial Map

Create a pictorial map of Italy. Draw 10 symbols that best represent the country. Complete the map key by listing your symbols and their meanings.

Map Key

Page 51

Italy

Name ________

Language

Use an encyclopedia, Italian dictionary, or another resource to help you complete these activities.

1. Write the correct numerals above the Italian number words. Give your source.

10 dieci	6 sei	2 due
8 otto	1 uno	9 nove
5 cinque	4 quattro	3 tre
7 sette	Source: ________	

2. In Italian, write the number words in the correct order. Add a comma between each number.
   uno, due, tre, quattro, cinque, sei, sette, otto, nove, dieci

Food

Refer to an Italian cookbook and an encyclopedia for these activities.

1. How do Italian foods vary by region? Give examples.
   Answers will vary.
2. On another sheet, draw and label 10 kinds of Italian pasta. Briefly explain the use of each.

Extension: Pretend that you are an Italian exchange student who wishes to prepare a special Italian meal for your American host family. Make a list of the dishes you will make and the ingredients you will need.

Page 52

Latvia

Name ______

Physical Features and General Information

1. On the map, draw a star to show the location of Latvia's capital. Write the city's name by the star.
2. Label the countries that border Latvia.
3. Label the Baltic Sea.
4. Draw and label the Western Dvina (Daugava) River.
5. In what year did Latvia gain its independence from the Soviet Union? 1991

6. The official language of Latvia is Latvian. Latvia's language is related to what ancient Indian language? Sanskrit
7. What is the area of Latvia? 24,749 sq. mi. 64,100 sq. km.
8. What is another name for Latvians? Letts They make up what percent of the population? 52% Name the other ethnic groups that make up Latvia's population. Russian, Belarusian, Polish, Ukrainian, Lithuanian, Jewish
9. What do Latvians do for recreation? basketball, soccer, attend ballet and theater, participate in choral singing
10. In the box, draw and color Latvia's flag.

Extension: Research religion in Latvia while the country was under Soviet control. Write two imaginary letters from a Latvian minister to his brother, one written before independence and one written after independence.

Page 53

Liechtenstein

Name ______

Physical Features

1. On the map, draw a star to mark the location of the capital of Liechtenstein. Write the city's name by the star.
2. Draw and label the river that runs along the west border of Liechtenstein.
3. Use the symbol ^^^ to mark the highest region of Liechtenstein. What is the name and the elevation of the country's highest peak? Vorder-Grauspitz 8,527 ft. ; 2,599m

4. Color the country's strip of farmland green and the mountain areas brown.
5. What country borders Liechtenstein on the west? Switzerland On the east? Austria Label these countries on the map.
6. Liechtenstein's area is only 62 sq. mi. or 160 sq. km.
7. What type of animal is raised on the farms in Liechtenstein? cattle What are the country's main manufactured products? crafts, precision instruments, cotton textiles, heating appliances, drugs
8. What type of climate would you find in Liechtenstein? mild for a mountain area What is the average temperature? 47° F What is the average precipitation? 35"/year Compare the average temperature and precipitation in Liechtenstein to the temperature and precipitation in your area. Find the difference between each. Answers will vary.

Extension: Imagine taking a boat ride down the Rhine River. Where would you stop along your route? What would you see?

Page 54

Liechtenstein

Name ______

History and Culture

1. In the box, draw and color the country's flag. Explain the meaning of the colors. blue - sky, red - glow of evening fires

2. What was the last war in which Liechtenstein fought? Seven Weeks' War In what year did this occur? 1866
3. Who has ruled the country since the early 1700s? Johann-Adam Liechtenstein and his descendants.
4. Tell what happened in Liechtenstein on each of these dates:
   - 1719 independence from Roman Empire
   - 1815 joined German Confederation
   - 1866 last war
   - 1868 has had no army since this date
5. In what ways are Liechtenstein's close ties with the Swiss evident? Swiss money; Switzerland operates its postal, telegraph, and telephone systems; Switz. represents L. in diplomatic relations
6. Briefly describe the lifestyle of the people of Liechtenstein. small villages, rural settings, homes are small, people wear traditional costumes, work in factories
7. What world-famous collection can be found in Vaduz? fine art collection Name some of the works that are a part of this collection. Pieter Bruegel, Botticelli, Rembrandt, Peter Paul Rubens In what way does the government use this collection? It makes and sells stamps of famous paintings.
8. What is the main religion of the people of Liechtenstein? Roman Catholic
9. What is the official language of the country? German

Page 55

Lithuania

Name ______

Physical Features and General Information

1. On the map, draw a star to mark the location of the capital of Lithuania. Write the city's name by the star.
2. Use a dot to mark four other cities on the map. Write each name by the correct dot.
3. Label the countries that border Lithuania.

4. Briefly describe Lithuania's land. The land consists of lowlands and gently sloping hills. It has many rivers and lakes.
5. What were four changes that took place in Lithuania during Soviet rule? Answers will vary.
6. In what year did Lithuania gain its independence from the Soviet Union? 1991
7. What are four of Lithuania's major industries? agriculture, chemicals, electrical equipment, fabricated metal products
8. What is a *daino*? It is an ancient Lithuanian song.
9. Describe a typical Lithuanian celebration. National costumes may be worn and traditional songs and dances may be performed.
10. In the box, draw and color Lithuania's flag. Explain each color. yellow - ripening grain, green - evergreen forests, red - blood shed for freedom

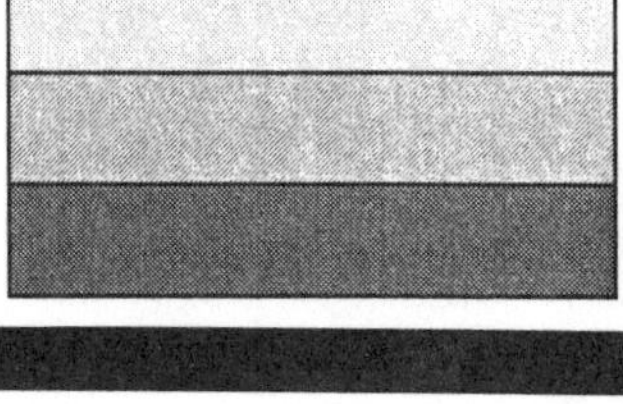

Page 56

Luxembourg

Name ____________

Physical Features

1. On the map, draw a star to mark the location of the capital of Luxembourg. Write the city's name by the star.
2. What is the population of the city of Luxembourg? 75,377
3. Draw and label the four rivers that run through Luxembourg.
4. Label the countries that border Luxembourg.
5. What is the highest point in Luxembourg? Buurgplatz

   Mark this point with a Λ on the map.
6. What are the two main land regions of Luxembourg? Write a brief description of each region.

   1) the Ardennes – in Northern Luxembourg, a part of a mountain range

   2) the Bon Pays – the rest of Luxembourg, a hilly, rolling plateau
7. What is the most valuable resource of Luxembourg? iron ore
8. What are Luxembourg's chief exports? iron and steel products
9. What is the average temperature in Luxembourg in January? 32° F

   in July? 63°F Compare Luxembourg's average temperatures to temperatures in your area. How much hotter/colder is it in these months in your area?

   Answers will vary.

Extension: Trace a map of Luxembourg onto a blank sheet of paper. Trace a map of the smallest U.S. state on top of this map in a different color. The maps should be roughly the same scale. List the areas of both. Which is bigger?

Page 57

Luxembourg

Name ____________

History and Culture

1. In the box, draw and color Luxembourg's flag. How were the colors of Luxembourg's flag chosen?

   They come from the country's coat of arms.

2. Who built the castle located on the site of the present-day city of Luxembourg?

   Count Siegfried

   In what year was it built? 963

   In the A.D. 300s, who built the fort in what is now the city of Luxembourg?

   Roman soldiers
3. Name four countries that have ruled Luxembourg. Spain, France, Austria, Netherlands
4. What World War II battle was fought in Luxembourg? When? The Battle of the Bulge; Dec., 1944
5. The Luxembourgers are considered "prosperous" people. Explain.

   They have a high standard of living, plentiful food, and great culture.
6. What are the main occupations of the people of Luxembourg? farmers, steel workers, high tech, international banking
7. What is the approximate population of Luxembourg? 386,000 (1995)
8. What is the primary religion of the country? Roman Catholic
9. What are some of the favorite foods of the people of Luxembourg? bean soup, pork, fish, saurkraut, rench fries, black pudding
10. Name the leading industry in Luxembourg. steel

Extension: Choose several dates in Luxembourg's history that you find interesting and make a historic time line.

Page 58

Luxembourg

Name ____________

Language

1. What are the country's official languages? French, German, Letzburgesch

   What is the everyday language of Luxembourg? Letzburgesch

   What languages are taught in the schools? French and German
2. Using a German dictionary or other resource, write the following words in German.

   river fluss mountain berg forest wald

   cattle vien grape weinbeere castle schloss
3. Since French is also used in Luxembourg, write the same six words in French.

   river de rivière mountain de la montagne forest forêt

   cattle bétail grape grain de raisin castle château

Extension: Design a travel guide for a tourist visiting several Luxembourg cities. Include types of transportation, points of interest, and the miles between cities. Try to find pictures or illustrations for your guide. Include both German and French phrases that a tourist might use while visiting.

Page 59

Macedonia

Name ____________

Physical Features and General Information

1. On the map, draw a star to mark the location of the capital of Macedonia. Write the city's name by the star.
2. Label the countries that border Macedonia.
3. Macedonia's landscape is filled with mountains.

   Most of the country lies on a plateau that is how many feet above sea level?

   2,000–3,000 ft.
4. List the name and height of Macedonia's highest point. Label it on the map.

   Mt. Korabit – 9,026 ft.

5. Describe Macedonia's climate. Mediterranean climate with hot, dry summers and cold winters with heavy snowfall
6. Macedonia's official language is Macedonian.
7. List four of Macedonia's ethnic groups. Albanians, Macedonian Slavs, Turks, Gypsies, Serbs

   Which one is the majority? Macedonian Slavs
8. Macedonia was part of Yugoslavia from 1945 to 1990. In 1990, the Communists lost control of the government and Macedonia declared its independence. However, many nations refused to recognize it as a n independent nation.
9. What percentage of all Macedonians live in cities? 55 %
10. Macedonian music shows influence from the Turks who ruled the region between which centuries? 1300's – 1900's
11. What is the *oro*? a type of circle dance
12. Why did/does Greece have a problem with Macedonia's name and status as a country?

    Its name and flag are linked to Greece's history and Macedonia will not change them.

Page 60

Malta

Name ______

Physical Features

1. On the map, draw a star to mark the location of Malta's capital. Write the city's name by the star.

2. Malta is an island country. Name the five islands that make up this country.
   Malta
   Comino
   Cominotto
   Filfla
   Gozo
3. Which of these islands are uninhabited?
   Cominotto
   Filfla
4. Label the body of water that surrounds Malta.
5. Read about the climate, average temperature, and rainfall in Malta. How is it similar or different from the area where you live? Answers will vary.
6. What is terrace farming? Why do you think this type of farming is used in Malta?
   It involves planting crops on wide flat rows on a hillside; it looks like a staircase. In Malta, terraced farming saves space, conserves water, and prevents erosion.

Extension: In the box, draw a diagram of a terrace farm.

Page 61

Malta

Name ______

History and Culture

1. In the box, draw and color the Maltese flag. Explain the meaning of the insignia on the flag.
   Replica of the George Cross medal awarded to Malta for bravery in WWII.

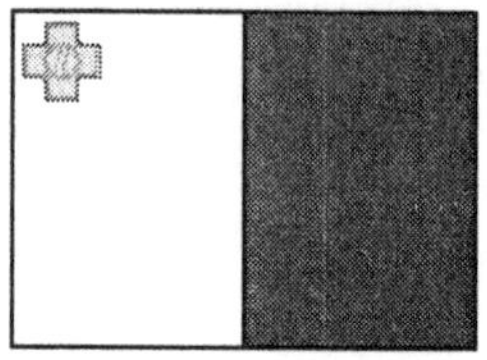

2. What is the Maltese national anthem? Innu Malti
3. Why was Malta of such great military significance in wartime?
   It had a strategic location and natural harbors.
4. Describe the role Malta played in World War II. It controlled the sea between Italy and Africa. Deep inlets concealed submarine bases.
5. What nation was the last to own Malta? Britain
   When did Malta become an independent country? 1964
6. About one-third of the Maltese people work in the dockyards. Why is this such an important business? Most of the goods needed by Malta must be imported.
7. What ancient relics have been found in Malta? Remains of the Stone and Bronze Ages, temples, tombs, and relics of the Phoenicians have been found in Malta.
8. How does Malta's school system compare with your country's?
   Answers will vary.

Extension: Write a short story that takes place during World War II in Malta's underground passages.

Page 62

Malta

Name ______

Language and Food

1. What are the official languages of Malta? Maltese and English
2. Why do you think the country of Malta, located between Italy and Africa, has English newspapers? Malta was previously held by Great Britain. Military influence by British during WWII also plays a role along with British tourists.
3. What are some of the crops grown in Malta? barley, cauliflower, citrus fruits, flowers, grapes, green peppers, onions, potatoes, tomatoes, wheat
4. Why must the people of Malta import most of their food?
   Farmland is scarce; much of the soil is rocky.
   What are the three main countries that export food products to Malta?
   Great Britain, Italy, Germany
   What types of foods are imported? fruit, grains, vegetables, meat
5. Find a recipe that might be used by the Maltese. Base your choice on Malta's location and the types of crops and animals grown or raised on their farms. Recipes will vary.
   Recipe: ______ Source: ______
   Ingredients: ______
   Preparation: ______
6. Name the countries that most likely influence Maltese cuisine.
   Italy, Great Britain, Germany — because of trade.

Page 63

Moldova

Name ______

Physical Features/General Information

1. On the map, draw a star to mark the location of Moldova's capital city. Write the name by the star.

2. Moldova is sandwiched between which two countries? Label these countries on the map.
   Ukraine and Romania
3. Moldova's land could be described as hilly.
4. Moldova has over 3,000 rivers, the main one being the Dnestr River.
   Draw and label it on the map.
5. Before belonging to the Soviet Union, Moldova belonged to what country? Romania
6. Like many other former Soviet-ruled countries, Moldova declared its independence in what year? 1991
7. What is Moldova's official language? Romanian
8. Why do you think Moldova's parliament ordered the Cyrillic (Russian) alphabet to be replaced by the Roman alphabet?
   Possible answer: As Soviets lost control, Moldovans wishing to emphasize independence, returned to the use of their traditional Roman alphabet.
9. Provide details about Moldova's population such as its density and distribution.
   Population: 4,350,000
   Most people live in rural villages. 47% live in urban areas
   In what occupation do most of the population work? farming

Extension: Research to find the Cyrillic alphabet. Write a short message using this alphabet.

Page 64

Monaco

Name

Physical Features and General Information

1. On the map, draw a star to mark the location of Monaco's capital city. Write the city's name by the star.
2. What country borders Monaco on three sides? *France*
   What borders Monaco on its remaining side? *the Mediterranean Sea*
3. Write the names of the four distinct parts of Monaco where they are located on the map.
4. What makes Monaco an important tourist resort? *It has a desirable climate and location on the French Riviera. It is known for its casinos, botanical gardens, and auto racing.*
5. Compare Monaco's size, in area, to the smallest U.S. state. *Rhode Island is 1,213 sq. mi. and 3,142 sq. km. Monaco is .75 sq. mi. and 1.95 sq. km.*
6. The principal language of Monaco is *French*. Most natives speak a dialect called *Monégasque*, which is related to *French* and *Italian*.
7. Colorful postage stamps are important to Monaco's economy. Design one for them illustrating one of their well-known attractions.

Stamp designs will vary.

Extension: Find brochures, travel posters, or other tourist information on Monaco. Display these in your classroom. Also, design and display a tourist map of Monaco showing these places: Cathedral of Monaco, Government Palace, Grand Theatre, Marine Museum, Museum of Fine Arts, Museum of Prehistoric Anthropology.

Page 65

Monaco

Name

History and Culture

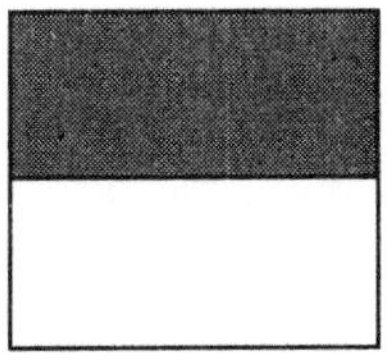

1. In the box, draw and color Monaco's flag with its correct colors.
2. What is Monaco's type of government? *principality*
   Explain briefly how this type of government works. *It is ruled by a prince; rule is passed down to the male heir.*
3. What important changes came when Monaco's constitution was revised in 1962? *Women were allowed to vote and the death penalty was abolished.*
4. What countries have ruled Monaco from 700 B.C. to the present? *Phoenicia, Spain, France, Italy*
5. Why has Monaco reclaimed land from the sea? *It needed beaches for the tourist trade and on which to build buildings.*
6. What effect do you think the French had on the cultural development of the people of Monaco? *Answers will vary.*
7. What are natives of Monaco called? *Monégasque*
8. Why have many people of other countries located to Monaco? *Except for French residents, there is no income tax.*
9. What is unique about the Princess Caroline Library? *Named for Prince Rainier and Grace Kelly's daughter, it specializes in children's literature.*

Extension: Pretend that you are a tour guide for the country of Monaco. Write a brief presentation to give your tourists as you travel from the Casino dEté down Princess Grace Avenue to the Palace of the Prince. Include information about Prince Rainier, Prince Albert, Princess Grace, and Princess Caroline.

Page 66

Netherlands

Name

Physical Features

1. On the map, draw two stars: one blue star to show the location of the capital of the Netherlands and one red star to show the seat of government. Print the city names by each star.
2. Label the countries and the sea that border the Netherlands.
3. Divide the map into its four main land regions. Color each region a different color. Set up a map key to show what region each color represents.
4. Two-fifths of the Netherlands was once covered with water. The people created polders to make this land usable. Explain *polders* and how they were created. *Polders were made by draining the land. Dikes were built and windmills and electric pumps were used to pump out the water. Canals carry water to the North Sea.*
5. What purposes do the canals serve? *Canals drain the land and serve as waterways.*
6. What region has the most productive farmland and the country's largest cities? *The Polders*
7. Briefly describe the country's climate. *It has a mild, damp climate. West winds from the North Sea warm the country in winter and cool it in the summer.*

Extension: Find information about the catastrophe in the delta area in 1953. Take notes and share this information with your classmates.

Page 67

Netherlands

Name

History and Culture

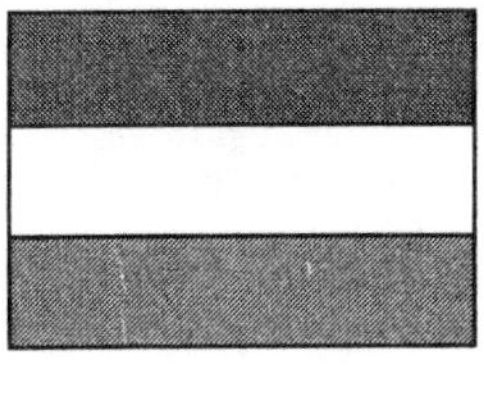

1. In the box, draw and color the flag. How did the flag change after 1630? *The top stripe changed from orange to red.*
2. Who controlled the Netherlands from 1516 to 1648? *the Spanish*
3. Why were the 1600s called the "Golden Age of the Netherlands"? *The country formed a large colonial empire; it became a major sea power; the Dutch were responsible for half of Europe's shipping.*
4. Tell what important event involving the United States took place in 1624. *The Dutch colonized New Netherland consisting of New York, New Jersey, Connecticut, and Delaware.*
5. How did the Netherlands recover after the devastation of World War II? *They rebuilt their country and re-established position in world trade and commerce.*
6. What are the main occupations of the Dutch? *Skilled work in electronic and chemical industry; agriculture; banking; trade; tourism*
7. How is the Netherlands's high school educational system different from that in your country? *It offers no general highschool program but various highschool programs aimed at particular career paths.*
8. Name several of the Netherlands's great painters. If possible, find illustrations of their works to show in class. *Pieter de Hooch, Frans Hals, Rembrandt, van Ruisdael, Vermeer, van Gogh, Mondrian*

Extension: Find a story or poem that tells about the dikes or canals of the Netherlands. Discuss with others why dikes and canals make interesting material for stories and poetry.

Page 68

Netherlands

Name ____________

Language

1. The Dutch language is part of what language group? Germanic
2. Use a dictionary, encyclopedia, or resource person to define these words:
   - kermis: carnival
   - Netherlands: low land
   - klompen: wooden shoe
   - Sinterklaas: Santa Claus
   - gezelligheid: friendship
   - yacht: large boat
3. Write several Dutch words that represent objects in the Netherlands. Give their English translations. Name the source where you found the information.
   Answers will vary.
4. What is the IJsselmeer? It is a fresh-water lake that was part of the Zuider Zee.

The Hague

1. Write three sentences that describe or tell about The Hague.
   Answers will vary.
2. Who contributed the funds to build The Hague's Peace Palace? Andrew Carnegie
   Why was the Peace Palace built? It was built as an international capital for world peace conferences.

Page 69

Norway

Name ____________

Physical Features and General Information

1. On the map, draw a star to mark the location of Norway's capital city. Write the capital's name by the star.
2. Label the Sogne Fiord.
3. Label the countries and the ocean that border Norway.
4. Use a ∧ to mark Norway's tallest mountain on the map. Label it.
5. Draw and label the Glåma River.
6. The full length of Norway's coastline is 13,267 miles. How does this compare to the distance around the world?
   It is half the distance around the world.

7. What is a fiord? It is a long, narrow inlet of the sea.
8. Name the two largest island groups off the Norway coast.
   Lofoten — Vesterålen
9. When and why did mining become an important economic activity in Norway?
   During the 1970s it produced petroleum and gas.
10. How does the social welfare system benefit Norway's people? National Insurance Act provides pensions, job retraining, aid for mothers, health care
11. Where is Lapland? Describe the clothing and housing of those who live there.
    It's located in the far North, above the Arctic Circle. Lapps are nomadic. They wear modern and traditional clothing made of wool and reindeer fur trimmed with bright cloth. They live in tents or simple houses.

Extension: Write a brief summary giving reasons for the mild climate along the western coast of Norway in winter and its cooler climate in summer.

Page 70

Norway

Name ____________

History and Culture

1. In the box, draw and color the flag.
2. How long ago were people living in Norway? 11,000 years ago
3. List three facts about the Viking period.
   Answers will vary.
4. How do the physical features of Norway affect the lifestyle of its people? Salmon caught in Norwegian waters; skiing, fishing, ice skating influenced livelihood and recreation.
5. What three Norwegian writers have won the Nobel Prize for Literature?
   Bjørnstjerne Bjørnson, Knut Hamsun, and Sigrid Undset
   Choose one of these writers and give the year and the name of the literary work that won the Nobel Prize.
   Answers will vary.
6. Tell what style of music Edvard Grieg composed. List a few of his compositions by title.
   He was a composer of symphonic music with a strongly nationalistic style. Titles will vary.
7. Explain how the educational system of Norway differs from the system in your country.
   Children must go to school beginning at age 7. College prepartion and vocational paths are offered.
8. Who was Henrik Ibsen? He was a playwright Why was he called the father of modern drama? He wrote realistic plays.
   List some of his works. The Warriors Barrow, Hedda Gabler, The Wild Duck, A Doll's House

Extension: Choose an event that greatly affected the economy of Norway. Share this information with your classmates. How would the country be different if this event had not happened or if it had had a different outcome?

Page 71

Poland

Name ____________

Physical Features and Government

1. On the map, draw a star to identify the location of the capital city of Poland. Write the capital's name by the star.
2. Name Poland's seven land areas.
   1) the Coastal Lowlands
   2) the Baltic Lakes Region
   3) the Central Plains
   4) the Polish Uplands
   5) the Carpathian Forelands
   6) the Sudetes Mountains
   7) the Western Carpathian Mountains

3. Which of these areas would you choose to live in? Why?
   Answers will vary.
4. On the map, draw and label these rivers: Vistula, Bug, Oder, and Warta.
5. Label the sea and the countries that border Poland.
6. What is Poland's most important natural resource? coal
7. Calculate the number of miles from New York City to Warsaw, Poland. 4,267
8. Poland is one of the world's leading producers of what two products?
   coal and silver
9. Poland's parliament is called the National Assembly. It is made up of two houses. The lower house, or Sejm, and the upper house, or Senate.
10. Who presently heads the Polish government? Lech Walesa
11. When was the first time free elections were held in Poland since the 1940s? 1989

Extension: Read about Lech Walesa. Share this information in a report or story.

Page 72

Poland

Name ______

History and Culture

1. In the box, draw and correctly color the flag of Poland.

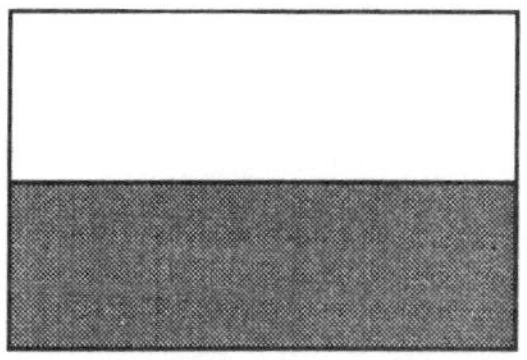

2. What is the national anthem and what does it mean? "Jeszcze Polska nie zaginela" ("Poland has not yet perished.")
3. When did Poland become an independent republic? 1918
4. Name four significant events in Poland's history that affected its world position. Answers will vary.
5. Explain how labor strikes in the 1980s affected Poland's work environment. better working conditions, free trade unions, some political reforms
6. What recreational activities are popular in Poland? soccer, track, cycling, camping, hiking, skiing, bridge
7. In what major way has the Poles' lifestyle changed since 1900? from an agricultural to a largely industrial nation; rural to urban
8. Why is the standard of living lower in Poland than in Western European countries? The country does not produce enough consumer goods.
9. What famous composer wrote music based on Polish dances? Chopin
10. Name three Poles who have won the Nobel Prize. Henryk Sienkiewicz, Wladyslaw Reymont, Czeslaw Milosz

Extension: Draw maps showing the partitioning that occurred in Poland in 1918, in 1939, and in 1945.

Page 73

Portugal

Name ______

Physical Features

1. On the map, draw a star to identify the location of Portugal's capital city. Write the city's name by the star.
2. Label the country and body of water that border Portugal.
3. Name Portugal's four main land regions.
   1) the Coastal Plains
   2) the Northern Tablelands
   3) the Central Range
   4) the Southern Tablelands

4. What is the *meseta*? It is the huge plateau that covers much of the Iberian Peninsula.
5. On the map, draw and label the three major rivers of Portugal.
6. Name at least three of Portugal's natural resources. building stone, coal, copper, forests, ocean fish
7. Use a ∧ to mark Portugal's highest point on the map. Name this point and give its elevation. Estrela - 6,539 ft.
8. On the map, draw a dot to mark the second largest Portuguese city. Write its name by the dot.
9. Where do the majority of Portugal's people live? rural villages often near coast.
10. Compare and contrast the lifestyles of the residents of Porto or Lisbon with a small town or village in Portugal. Answers will vary.

Extension: Describe a typical Portuguese farm. Compare it to a typical large midwestern U.S. farm.

Page 74

Portugal

Name ______

History and Culture

1. In the box, draw and correctly color the flag. What do its colors signify? green - hope, red - blood of the country's heroes

2. What is the national anthem? "A Portuguesa"
3. What were the first Portuguese inhabitants called? Iberians
4. Name three Portuguese explorers of the 1400s and 1500s. Dias, de Gama, Cabral

   Pick one and tell about his voyage. Answers will vary.
5. What are four favorite Portuguese recreational activities? folksinging, bullfights, soccer, picnics, walks
6. How do Portuguese bullfights differ from those of Spain and Latin America? Bulls are not killed.
7. Portuguese architects used ornate designs called *Manueline* in buildings. Give an example of this art form and note for whom it was named. Church in Tomar, named for Manuel I, ruler from 1495-1521.
8. Name the most famous literary work of Portugal's golden age. "Os Lusíadas"

   Who wrote this epic poem? Luiz de Camões

   Tell briefly the main theme of the poem. Praise of Portugal's historical accomplishments and heroes.

Extension: Pretend you were a crewmember for one of the famous Portuguese explorers. Write a journal entry that illustrates your part in an exploration.

Page 75

Portugal

Name ______

Language

1. What is the official language of Portugal? Portuguese

   It is often referred to as one of the romance languages. Tell why. It developed from Latin.
2. What is the basic unit of money in Portugal? Portuguese Escudo
3. How many principal Portuguese dialects are there? four
4. How did the language change after 1943? "f" was substituted for "ph," "t" for "th," "i" for "y."
5. How did Portugal get its name? It comes from "Portus Cale," the original name for the town of Porto
6. Tell how these three words relate to music: *chulas, viras, fados.* chulas and viras - lively songs; fados - sad songs

Miracle of Fátima

1. Where in Portugal is the village of Fátima located? west central
2. What important event reportedly occurred there in 1917? The Virgin Mary was believed to have appeared to three children tending sheep.

   How did this affect the future of Fátima? Thousands pilgrimage to Fatima annually.
3. Read about the miracle at Fátima. List important details about this story. Answers will vary.

Page 76

Romania

Name ____________

Physical Features

1. On the map, draw a star to mark the location of Romania's capital city. Write the city's name by the star.
2. Using a red pencil, marker, or pen, draw in the six land regions of Romania and label them.
3. Draw the Danube River using a blue pen or pencil.
4. Label the countries and body of water that border Romania.

5. Is Romania larger or smaller in size than the state or province where you live? By how much?
   Answers will vary.
6. List four of Romania's natural resources.
   fertile soil, forests, bauxite, coal, copper, gold, petroleum
7. Imagine you are vacationing in Romania and traveling through each of its six regions. Write about your travels and include details about each of the regions. Use the back of this page, if necessary.
   Answers will vary.

Page 77

Romania

Name ____________

History and Culture

1. In the box, draw and color Romania's flag in the correct colors.

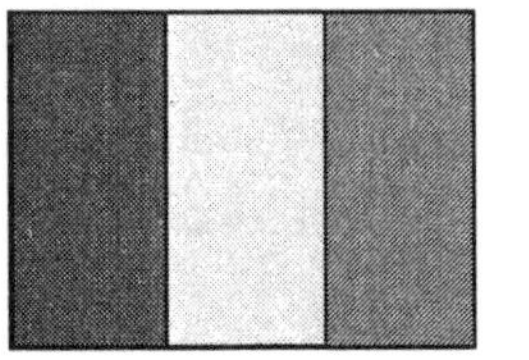

2. How did Romania get its name?
   It means "Land of the Romans" because ancient Rome occupied it
3. With whom did Romania join forces during World War I?
   France, Great Britain, and other Allies
4. Romania was a Soviet satellite. Define *Soviet satellite.* A country controlled by the U.S.S.R.
5. What is another spelling of Romania? Rumania
6. Who are Gypsies? They are groups of wandering people who live all over the globe. They may originate from India.
7. Look up *Dracula*. In what region of Romania does this story take place? Transylvania
8. What are some differences between a state farm and a collective farm?
   state farm - owned and operated by government
   collective farm - owned and operated by the community; they have older equipment.

   How are Romanian farms changing? More are privately owned.
9. Why is the Romanian language unique? It is the only Eastern European language that comes from Latin.
10. Rural Romanians decorate their cottages using hand-crafted rugs and plates.

Extension: Research Nicolae Ceausescu. Write a mock newspaper account of his last days in Romania.

Page 78

Russia

Name ____________

Physical Features

1. On the map, draw a star to show the location of Russia's capital city. Write its name by the star.
2. Label the following on the map above.

Caspian Sea	Ob River	Kara Sea
Black Sea	Volga River	Arctic Ocean
Barents Sea	Lena River	Bering Sea
Lake Baikal	Yenisey River	Sea of Okhotsk
Ural Mountains	all the bordering countries	

3. What is permafrost? How much of this country is covered by it?
   It is permanently frozen ground. Almost 50%.
4. Where does most of this region's rainfall occur? the European Plain
5. List four of Russia's natural resources.
   Coal, iron ore, timber, petroleum, fish, fertile soil in some areas, platinum-group metals, hydroelectric power.
6. What boundary do the Ural Mountains form? They separate European Russia from Asian.
7. On another sheet, describe either Russia's four zones or its five land regions.

Extension: Plan a trip to Russia. Outline your journey in pencil on the map above and tell a few interesting facts about four of the places you visited.

Page 79

Russia

Name ____________

General Information

1. What is Russia's basic unit of money? ruble
2. Do 75 percent of Russia's people live in urban or rural areas? urban
3. Why is there a severe housing shortage in Russian cities?
   In the 1930's large numbers of Russians moved to cities. During WWII bombs destroyed houses. Dire economic conditions prevented enough new housing from being built.
4. Describe the problems many people have living in Moscow.
   Families share kitchens and bathrooms.
   Extended families often live is small apartments.
5. The country's official language, Russian, is written in the Cyrillic alphabet.
6. Research the Russian alphabet and copy it here.
   АБВГДЕЁЖЗИЙКЛМНОПРСТУФХЦЧШЩЪ
   Ъ Ы Ь Э Ю Я
   See encyclopedia for Roman equivalents.
7. What are some popular Russian dishes? borscht (beet soup), piroshki (stuffed dumplings), beef Stroganoff
8. Define *sovkhozy* and *kolkhozy*. sovkhozy - state-controlled farm
   kolkhozy - managed in part by farmers, these farms are partly controlled by the government.

Extension: Research Catherine the Great. Pretend first that you were a famous Russian composer and second that you were a poor serf. Describe what life would have been like under Catherine's rule for each of these two people.

Page 80

Russia

Name

History and Culture

1. In the box, draw and correctly color the flag.

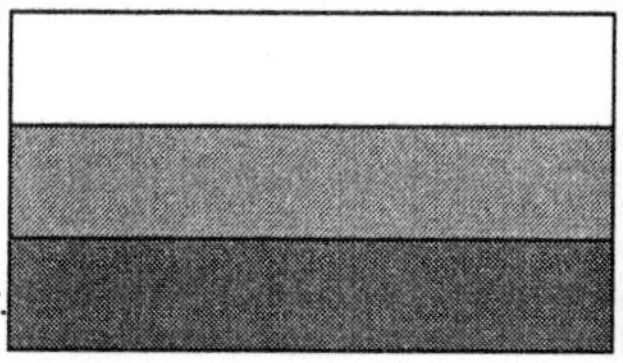

2. What happened to the Soviet Union in 1991? How did this affect Russia?
The Soviet Union collapsed. Russia set up a new political and legal apparatus.
3. What is a czar? A czar was a Russian emperor who had total control.
4. Who was Ivan the Terrible? He was Russia's first czar.
Describe him. He was a cruel, suspicious, insane ruler who set up a secret police. He killed his own son.
5. What Russians have won the Nobel Prize for literature? List one title of a famous work written by each.
Sholokhov, Pasternak, Solzhenitsyn, Brodsky (Russian born) Answers will vary.
6. Who was Tchaikovsky? He was one of the world's great composers.
List two of his works. Possible answers: "The Nutcracker Suite" "Romeo and Juliet"
7. For many centuries, Russian artists produced icons. What is an *icon*?
Icons are religious paintings produced from the late 900's to the 1600's.
8. Name two famous Russian ballet companies.
Bolshoi Theater Ballet; Kirov Ballet
9. Russia is known for what type of architecture? Byzantine

Extension: Choose an event, movement, or important figure from Russia's past to research and study. Share this information with your class in the form of a report, play, story, art activity, or project of your choice.

Page 81

San Marino

Name

Physical Features

1. On the map, draw a star to mark the location of the capital city of San Marino. Write the city's name by the star.

2. What country surrounds San Marino?
Italy
3. On what mountain does San Marino lie? Mt. Titano
Draw a ∧ to mark the highest peak. Label it.
4. What structure surrounds the city of San Marino?
A high stone wall surrounds the city.
5. What parts of the capital city's wall are symbols of the country? The towers connecting the walls of the city.
6. Is San Marino the oldest or newest republic in the world? oldest
7. What is San Marino's total area? 24 sq. mi. (61 sq. km.)
8. What is its approximate population? 23,000 (1995)
9. What do San Marino's people have in common with the people of northern Italy?
They speak Italian, practise Catholocism, and use Italian lira.
10. Describe the occupations of most San Marino people.
They work in tourist industry, in stone quarries, make leather, work in agriculture.
11. What makes San Marino an attractive place to visit?
The mountaintop capital has beautiful views and is filled with ancient and medieval architecture.

Extension: San Marino is known for its beautiful postage stamps. After reading about its culture, design a new stamp for it.

Page 82

Slovakia

Name

Physical Features and General Information

1. On the map, draw a star to identify the location of the capital city of Slovakia. Write its name by the star.
2. Label the five countries that border Slovakia.

3. What are the three major mountain ranges in Slovakia?
1) the White Carpathians
2) the Little Carpathians
3) the High Tatras
4. Why was the former Czechoslovakia split into Slovakia and the Czech Republic?
Czechs and Slavs could not agree on important governmental and economic issues.
5. What happened in 1989 and how did it affect the former Czechoslovakia?
Czechs and Slavs protested Communist control and put non-Communists in power.
6. Name the three population groups in Slovakia.
Slovak, Hungarian, Ukrainian, Gypsy, Czech, Russian, German, Polish
Who forms Slovakia's largest minority? Hungarians
7. Is the Slovakian standard of living higher or lower than most former Communist European countries? higher
8. What do many city families own? an automobile, television, washing machine, and a refrigerator

Extension: Pretend that tension exists among the ethnic groups living in your neighborhood in Slovakia. To foster good will, your family has decided to host a party at which each family brings an ethnic dish. List on another sheet the three ethnic groups along with the dish they might bring. Give the recipe for each dish.

Page 83

Slovenia

Name

Physical Features and General Information

1. On the map, draw a star to show the location of Slovenia's capital. Write its name by the star.

2. Label the countries that border Slovenia.
3. What type of landform covers most of the country? mountains
4. Label the Julian Alps with ⋀⋀. What is the name and height of the country's highest point?
Mount Triglav
9,393 feet
2,863 meters
5. What is the *Karst*? It is a limestone region of caves and underground channels.
6. What is the country's official language? Slovenian
7. Slovenia was once part of Yugoslavia, but declared its independence in 1991.
8. Slovenia's major group of people are called Slovene.
9. Who is considered the father of Slovenian literature? Primož Trubar
For what is he known? religious works and for translating the New Testament into Slovenian
10. In what two areas are most Slovenians employed?
manufacturing and service industry
11. If you visited Slovenia, what would you like to see?
Answers will vary.

Extension: Research Slovenia's *Kurenti* festival. Design and make a construction paper animal mask to be used at a *Kurenti* festival.

Page 84

Spain

Name ______

Physical Features and General Information

1. On the map, draw a star to mark the location of Spain's capital city. Write the city's name by the star.
2. Label the three countries and the sea and ocean that border Spain.
3. On the map, draw the boundaries of the seven major land regions and label each one.
4. What is Spain's area in square miles and square kilometers?
   194,885 sq. miles
   504,750 sq. kilometers
5. On the map, draw and label Spain's two longest rivers.
6. Mark the second largest city with a dot and then write its name.

7. What is Spain's most important natural resource? iron ore
8. Research the Canary Islands. How did they get their name? From the Latin "canis." Large, fierce dogs were found living on the islands.
9. List three facts about the Balearic Islands. Give your source.
   Answers will vary.

   Source(s): ______ Page(s): ______
10. What natural boundary separates Spain and France? the Pyrenees Mtns.

Extension: Plan a trip to Spain. Since it is such a large country, you have time to visit only four places. Trace your route on a copy of a map of Spain. Below the map, list and describe your stops. On the map, write the number of miles between consecutive points on your journey. Tell why these places were chosen.

Page 85

Spain

Name ______

History

1. In the box, draw and color Spain's flag with its correct colors.

2. What is the national anthem? "Marcha Royal" or "Royal March"
3. What famous non-Spanish explorer started a great age of exploration and conquest for Spain?
   Columbus
   When did he do this? late 1400s
4. Name two other explorers of this time and list one accomplishment for each.
   Answers will vary.
5. What was the Spanish Inquisition? It was a Spanish court established in 1480 that imprisoned or killed those suspected of not following Catholocism.
6. What caused Spain to lose the empire it had acquired in the 1500s? wars, heavy spending, bad weather in battle, poor management
7. What was the Spanish Armada? What happened to it in 1588?
   It was a powerful fleet of ships defeated by England in 1588.
8. What kind of ruler was Francisco Franco? How long did he rule?
   He was a dictator known for restricting freedoms. He ruled from 1939-1975.
9. When did Spain begin to establish a democracy? 1975, after Franco's death.

Extension: Read about Spain's role in the American Revolutionary War. Write a letter, detailing Spain's war strategy, from an imaginary Spanish general to George Washington.

Page 86

Spain

Name ______

Culture

1. Why can ancient Roman ruins be found in parts of Spain?
   Romans controlled Spain for 400 years.
2. Describe a typical Spanish workday for city workers.
   Three-hour lunch break; work until 7:00 p.m.
3. What is a *paseo*? How does it fit in with the Spanish lifestyle? It is a walk, usually taken in the evening. Most Spanish people regularly take a paseo.
4. How does life in the country differ from that of the city? no 3-hr. lunches, use donkey for transportation or travel on foot, wear informal clothing, have a lower standard of living.
5. Name two important sporting events in Spain. bullfighting, soccer
6. Spain is rich in artistic traditions. Name several famous artists from Spain.
   El Greco, Murillo, Velázque, Goya, Picasso, Dali, Gris, Miró, Tàpies
   Choose one artist on which to research and report.
7. Miguel de Cervantes, a Spanish author, wrote what literary masterpiece? Don Quixotic
   What is the main theme of this literary work? Possible answer: It depicts a modern man attempting to live by standards of chivalry in a modern world.
8. Read about the music of Spain. Name three world-famous Spanish dances.
   bolero, fandango, flamenco

   Find tapes or recordings of the kinds of music that accompanies these dances and share them with classmates.

Extension: Read about Madrid and Barcelona. As an art project, create tourist brochures for these two cities. Include places of interest, historical information, places to dine, and various kinds of recreation and entertainment. Try to include some Spanish words in your brochure. Include illustrations.

Page 87

Spain

Name ______

Language

Use a Spanish-English dictionary or encyclopedia to complete the activities below.

1. Write the Spanish words for the numerals one through ten.
   uno, dos, tres, cuatro, cinco, seis, siete, ocho, nueve, diez
2. Give the meanings of the following Spanish words:

siesta	bueno	madre	gato
nap	good	mother	cat
mucho	**gazpacho**	**escuela**	**casa**
much	cold soup	school	house

3. Find two or three advertisements or an article written in Spanish. On another sheet, note and report the words that are similar in both languages. Then have these translated by a Spanish-speaking person.

Food

1. List several foods or drinks we consume that originated in Spain. Use a Spanish cookbook or dictionary if necessary.
   paella, sangria, gazpacho, tapas
2. Why is seafood a staple food in Spain? It is inexpensive and plentiful.
3. Find a recipe for *paella*. Write it on a card to share with others.
4. At what time do urban-dwelling Spanish eat the evening meal? 10-11 PM
   What activities do they often do before and after the meal? They take walks.

Extension: As a class or family project, plan a meal including only Spanish cuisine. Credit your source for recipes and food ideas.

Page 88

Sweden

Name

Physical Features

1. On the map, draw a star to mark the location of Sweden's capital city. Write the city's name by the star.
2. Mark with a • and label three other large cities.
3. Label the countries and the sea and gulf that border Sweden.
4. Name and briefly describe Sweden's four main land regions.
   1) the Mountain Range – northern, treeless, glaciers
   2) the Inner Northland – hilly forests, rivers, few people
   3) the Swedish Lowland – populated, fertile plains
   4) the South Swedish Highland – rocky upland, forests

5. Draw and label on the map the two largest lakes in Sweden.
6. What are Sweden's most important natural resources? timber, iron ore, water power, rich farmland
7. How does Sweden compare in area to the other European countries? It is one of the largest.
8. How does its population compare? It is the least densely populated.
9. Research both Sweden's climate and its recreational activities. Tell what time of year you would choose to visit, where you would go, and what activities you would do once there. Answers will vary.
10. Sweden is considered a Scandinavian country along with which of its neighbors? Norway

Page 89

Sweden

Name

History

1. In the box, draw and correctly color Sweden's flag. When was it first used? mid 1400s

2. What is the national anthem? "Du gamla, du fria, du fjällhöga nord" ("Thou ancient, thou free, thou mountain-crowned north")
3. Where did the Swedish Vikings explore? East of Sweden to the Black and Caspian Seas
4. In early history, what countries made up the Union of Kalmar? Norway, Denmark, and Sweden
5. Who was Gustavus Vasa? What did he do? He was a Swedish noble who broke away from the Union in 1523. He became king of independent state, established Lutheranism as state religion, etc.
6. Research types of Swedish occupations from the early 1800s to the present. Then write short descriptions of workers from three different time periods. For each worker, include the time period, a made-up Swedish name, his/her occupation, and what work conditions were like. Answers will vary.
7. What chemical explosive was invented by Alfred Nobel? dynamite
   When was it patented? 1867

Extension: Research important dates in Sweden's history. On a separate sheet of paper, give the dates and historical events that also involved Norway and Denmark.

Page 90

Sweden

Name

Culture

1. Sweden has one of the highest standards of living in the world. Give several reasons why this is true. It has prosperous industries, government funds for medical, educational, and housing needs, etc.
2. What is the basic unit of money in Sweden? Swedish Krona
3. What are Sweden's chief winter sports? hockey, cross-country skiing
4. Describe the Vasa Race. It is a 55-mile cross-country ski race held each March from Sälen to Mora.
5. Who was the first Swedish writer to win the Nobel Prize? Selma Lagerlöf
   What children's book did she write? The Wonderful Adventures of Nils.
   If possible, locate this book and share it with your class.
6. List several ways in which the Lapps who live in Sweden's far north differ from most other Swedes. more traditional clothing, some travel from place to place and sleep in tents, live off land.
7. What is *smörgasbörd*? It is a large buffet of hot and cold foods.

Draw two smörgasbörds below, one depicting Swedish foods and one showing your favorites.

Pictures will vary.	Pictures will vary.

Extension: Research Swedish holidays. Write reports on St. Lucia Day and Midsummer's Eve. Include illustrations.

Page 91

Switzerland

Name

Physical Features

1. On the map, draw a star to mark the location of Switzerland's capital city. Write its name by the star.
2. Mark the cities of Geneva and Zurich with a heavy dot. Write each name by the correct dot.
3. Label the countries that border Switzerland.
4. What are the three main land regions of Switzerland?
   1) the Jura Mtns.
   2) the Swiss Plateau
   3) the Swiss Alps

5. Draw and label the Rhine River, the Rhône River, the Inn River, and the Ticino River.
6. Draw Lake Constance and Lake Geneva. Color Lake Constance blue and label Lake Geneva.
7. What is Switzerland's greatest natural resource? How does this resource benefit Switzerland? Water power is used to run Switzerland's many industries.
8. What causes the wide variety of temperatures in Switzerland? extreme altitude variations
   Make a bar graph or a chart showing temperature variations in the Alps compared with the Swiss Plateau.
9. Research the Matterhorn. On the back of this page, write a comparison in location, elevation, and general area topography with Mt. McKinley in the U.S.
10. Bicycling, target shooting, and bobsledding are three popular Swiss activities. Tell where in the country and during what time of year you would do each one.
    bicycling: Answers will vary.
    target shooting:
    bobsledding:

Extension: Research the Swiss Alps. Write a report giving important facts that visitors and tourists would like to know. Create a three-dimensional design of a mountain resort in the Alps.

Page 92

Switzerland

Name ____________

History

1. In the box, draw and color Switzerland's flag. What does the cross represent?
Christianity

2. List five groups of people who occupied what is now Switzerland between 100 B.C. and A.D. 800.
Celts
Romans
Alemannians
Burgundians
Franks
3. What is Switzerland's unit of money? franc Give two reasons why people all over the world do their banking in Switzerland. The money is very safe because of Swiss neutrality. It is also private.
4. What was the Perpetual Covenant? It was a defense agreement signed by three regions in 1291 which unified to form beginnings of Switz.
5. What world-renowned organization was founded in 1863 by Jean Henri Dunant?
Red Cross
6. When did Switzerland first establish a policy of neutrality? early 1500s
7. Give several reasons why Switzerland was able to maintain neutrality throughout World War I and World War II. Other countries needed their transportation system through the mountains
8. Do you agree with Switzerland's policy of neutrality? Why, or why not?
Answers will vary.

Extension: Research John Calvin. Write a paragraph from an imaginary diary he might have kept in Geneva in 1538.

Page 93

Switzerland

Name ____________

Culture

1. What special types of music are unique to Switzerland? Yodeling and playing the alphorn
Find tapes or records of Swiss music to bring to the class and play.
2. Draw an alphorn. Explain its construction. What is it used for?
It's a long tube-shaped instrument made of long wooden staves tightly bound together with birchbark to be air tight.
It is used by herders to call cattle in.
Pictures will vary.
3. Would you say music plays an important part in the life of the Swiss? Why?
Answers will vary.
4. What are two well-known Swiss children's classics? Who are the authors?
Heidi by Johanna Spyri
Swiss Family Robinson by the Wyss family
5. What is *hornussen*? It is a traditional Swiss game played with rackets, a club, and a disk.
6. Switzerland is a thriving industrial nation. Name three important goods they manufacture.
cheese, chocolate, electrical equipment, precision instruments, watches
7. What is *Dadaism*? It was an art movement founded in Zurich based on deliberate irrationality.
8. In what area do most of the Swiss people live? Many live in small cities. 2/5 live in rural areas. The others live in large cities.
Draw a picture of a Swiss chalet on another sheet.

Extension: Swiss watchmaking is world famous. Research this topic. You may wish to consult a local jeweler. Write several reasons why watchmaking is important to the Swiss people.

Page 94

Switzerland

Name ____________

Language

1. What are the official languages of Switzerland? German, French, Italian
2. Write the word "Switzerland" in the official languages of the country.
German- Schweiz French- Suisse Italian- Svizzera
3. What are the national languages? The three official plus Romansh
4. Define these words:

Helvitia	Landsgemeinde
Switzerland	open air meeting
Schwyzerdütsch	Emmentaler
Swiss- German	Swiss cheese

5. Write 10 words you think a tourist might need to know while touring Switzerland. Since three languages are spoken—French, German, and Italian—write the words in all three languages. Give your sources.

English	French	German	Italian
Answers will vary.			

Sources: ____________

Page 95

Turkey

Name ____________

Physical Features

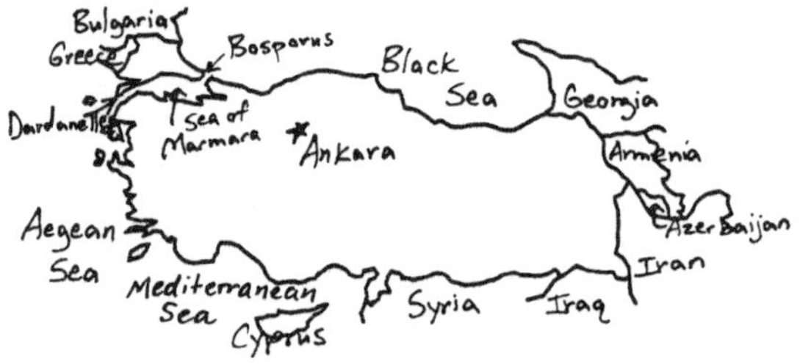

1. On the map, draw a star to show the location of Turkey's capital. Write the city's name by the star.
2. Turkey is located on which two continents? Asia and Europe
3. Name the part of Turkey that is in Europe. Thrace
4. On the map, label the two major seas and the countries that border Turkey.
5. Label the Bosporous, the Sea of Marmara, and the Dardanelles. What are these three bodies of water called? the Straits Describe their importance to Turkey.
Turkey, by controlling these waters, has been able to regulate the movement of ships between the Black Sea and Med. Sea.
6. Research Istanbul. Tell why its location is unique and describe old and new sections.
Istanbul is on both European and Asian continents. Descriptions will vary.
7. What are Turkey's eight major land regions?
1) the Northern Plains 2) the Western Valleys 3) the Southern Valleys 4) the Western Plateau 5) the Eastern Plateau 6) the Northern Mountains 7) the Southern Mts. 8) the Mesopotamian Lowlands
Study one land region or feature thoroughly. Present an oral report on that region or physical feature.

Page 96